If you're not familiar with Sophie Hudson already, you're about to find out why all of us who know her want to be her best friend. Whatever your love language, Sophie can speak it. If you need to laugh, she's your girl, but don't be shocked to find yourself moved to tears minutes later. She's all the things you love most in a woman of God. Have a blast with her!

BETH MOORE
New York Times bestselling author and speaker

This is Jerry Seinfeld in a skirt and a huge heart for Jesus. This is laugh-out-loud, hold-your-side funny. This is one unstoppable book—once you start reading, there's no stopping!

ANN VOSKAMP
Author of the *New York Times* bestseller *One Thousand Gifts: A Dare to Live Fully Right Where You Are*

Sophie Hudson has managed to capture all the heart and humor of growing up Southern in *A Little Salty to Cut the Sweet*. I devoured this book—I laughed out loud, I cried, I smiled, I talked back. For the first time in my life, I've found a book I wish every woman in my family could read together. There isn't a woman, no matter where she is from, who won't connect with the heart of this book. But the Southern women? They will feel it deep in their souls. That's the kind of book this is—the kind you read and feel and love and share.

ANNIE F. DOWNS
Author of *Perfectly Unique*

The very first blog I ever read was Sophie's *BooMama* blog, and I have read it every day since for the last six years. Her writing style keeps me coming back with her mix of HILARIOUS stories and the ability to make everyday things interesting. Sophie is the epitome of all that is Southern, and her writing brings that familiarity with it that makes you nod your head and say, "Uh-huh" and "Yes" if you were raised anywhere in the Southern states. *A Little Salty to Cut the Sweet* has made me laugh until I cried and has made me a little nostalgic for my family and childhood. It was everything I had hoped it would be and more!

KELLY STAMPS
Author of the kellyskornerblog.com

Well, it's official: I'm in love with this book. Sophie Hudson is hilariously appreciative of her very Southern roots, and she shares tales of all the experiences (and the lovably eccentric relatives!) that shaped her. Threads of love, family, and faith hold the stories together . . . but it's Sophie's laugh-at-life humor that sings forth from every page. She writes as if you're sitting on her front porch drinking a tall glass of sweet tea, and it's impossible not to come away from each chapter without feeling like you know her a little better. I can't remember the last time I had this much fun reading a book.

REE DRUMMOND
#1 *New York Times* bestselling author of *The Pioneer Woman Cooks*

A LITTLE SALTY
to Cut the Sweet

a little SALTY to cut the Sweet

SOPHIE HUDSON

author of BooMama blog

Tyndale House Publishers, Inc.
Carol Stream, Illinois

Visit Tyndale online at www.tyndale.com.

TYNDALE and Tyndale's quill logo are registered trademarks of Tyndale House Publishers, Inc.

A Little Salty to Cut the Sweet: Southern Stories of Faith, Family, and Fifteen Pounds of Bacon

Copyright © 2013 by Sophie Hudson. All rights reserved.

Embroidery by Soledad Nuñez. Copyright by Tyndale House Publishers, Inc. All rights reserved.

Cover background pattern copyright © Bill Noll/iPhoto. All rights reserved.

Floral illustration copyright © yewkeo/iStockphoto. All rights reserved.

Author photograph by Cam Cowan, copyright © 2012. All rights reserved.

Designed by Jacqueline L. Nuñez

Edited by Stephanie Rische

Published in association with William K. Jensen Literary Agency, 119 Bampton Court, Eugene, Oregon 97404.

Unless otherwise indicated, all Scripture quotations are taken from *The Holy Bible*, English Standard Version® (ESV®), copyright © 2001 by Crossway, a publishing ministry of Good News Publishers. Used by permission. All rights reserved.

Scripture quotations marked NIV are taken from the Holy Bible, *New International Version,*® *NIV.*® Copyright © 1973, 1978, 1984, 2011 by Biblica, Inc.™ Used by permission of Zondervan. All rights reserved worldwide. www.zondervan.com.

Scripture quotations marked *The Message* are taken from *The Message* by Eugene H. Peterson, copyright © 1993, 1994, 1995, 1996, 2000, 2001, 2002. Used by permission of NavPress Publishing Group. All rights reserved.

Library of Congress Cataloging-in-Publication Data

Hudson, Sophie.
    A little salty to cut the sweet : Southern stories of faith, family, and fifteen pounds of bacon / Sophie Hudson.
    pages cm
    ISBN 978-1-4143-7566-3 (pbk.)
    1. Hudson, Sophie—Anecdotes. 2. Hudson, Sophie—Family—Anecdotes. 3. Hudson, Sophie—Childhood and youth—Anecdotes. 4. Mississippi—Biography—Anecdotes. 5. Families—Mississippi—Anecdotes. 6. Christian life—Mississippi—Anecdotes. 7. Mississippi—Social life and customs—Anecdotes. 8. Southern States—Biography—Anecdotes. 9. Southern States—Social life and customs—Anecdotes. I. Title.
    CT275.H66727A3 2013
    976.2'064092—dc23
    [B]   2012049653

Printed in the United States of America

19	18	17	16	15	14	13
7	6	5	4	3	2	

For Papaw Davis, who always told the best stories

THESE ARE JUST SOME OF THE CHARACTERS IN MY FAMILY TREE

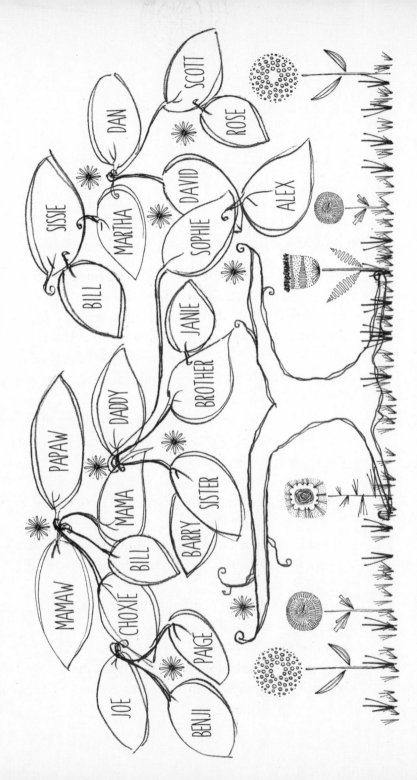

CONTENTS

A LITTLE LITERARY DISCLAIMER

THESE STORIES ARE TRUE—for the most part. I mean, you're reading my perspective on these true-for-the-most-part stories, and my perspective may differ from other people's. I think it's good to remember that. Plus, every once in a while I changed details and names because, well, it seemed like the right thing to do—lest I start some sort of family feud, you understand.

I also changed the names of some towns and altered some locations. Real life happens all over the place, and since I didn't want you to need a map in order to follow along, I consolidated the action to a few towns that exist only in my imagination. From that perspective, I guess the stories are 90 percent true-*ish* as opposed to 100 percent absolutely true.

I know. I'm overexplaining. It's what I do when I'm trying to make sure I'm covering all my storytelling bases.

There's a chance, I guess, that you'll find yourself wondering why I don't chronicle some big family falling-out, why we never seem to argue or disagree or fuss, so let me assure you that we most definitely do all of the above. You know that old Keith Whitley song called "I'm No Stranger to the Rain"? Well, we're

no strangers to the drama. I will say, however, that my grandparents set a high standard in terms of how they expected us to
treat each other, so even when we're aggravated, we're much more
apt to talk about it than to storm out of a room. On top of that,
this book is not meant to be An Airing of the Grievances; it's
meant to be a celebration of family.

Consider yourself warned that I may have been prone to some
exaggeration and embellishment every once in a while, but that
probably goes without saying, since I'm Southern and all.

Don't roll your eyes, people. *It's in my blood.*

Because I'm Crazy about My People

ONE OF THE GREAT BLESSINGS of my life is that I grew up in a family of storytellers. Some of my earliest memories involve sitting in Mamaw and Papaw Davis's den while my mama, my aunt, and their cousins took turns telling tales. The stories always featured real people and real-life events—like, for instance, Uncle Herman and Aunt Elsie, or one of the Keenans who lived down the road, or their cousin Tom Alex (pronounced "Ellec," a peculiar Mississippi pronunciation that puzzles me to this day)—and they were always hilarious.

What the stories were *not* was mean spirited. And there was never any profanity. In fact, the liveliest the language ever got was when my sweet Papaw would react to something by saying, "Well, I'll be John Brown." I had no idea who John Brown was, of course, but that's sort of beside the point. Because as I sat and listened to my mama imitate her uncle Owen and heard my aunt howl with laughter over something that had happened at the Moss Rose General Store, I learned very quickly that a good story doesn't require "all that foul language," as Mama might say. And with the exception of an unfortunate season in my early twenties when I regularly experimented with all the curse words in all their various forms, I've remembered the lesson.

Way back in ye olden days of 2005, I was the mama of a two-year-old and, according to my husband, a person who might benefit from a creative outlet that didn't involve Elmo, *Veggie Tales*, or *Blue's Clues*. I'd been reading blogs for a couple of years, and one night while I sat in the rocking chair in our guest room and watched our little guy play in the tub, I decided I was going to start one of those blog things and maybe try to get back in the swing of writing.

I had been a habitual journal keeper from my early teens until my late twenties, but after I got married, I abandoned the writing in favor of some fairly obsessive housekeeping and decorating. After all, it's tough to commit to keeping a journal when you're repainting your bedroom for the fifth time in a year and scouring T. J. Maxx and Marshalls for the latest shower curtain shipment. As a wise philosopher once said, "Discounted linens wait for no woman."

But that night in the guest room, I realized that I was ready to write again. I *needed* to write again. And I figured that if two or three people wanted to hop on the wide-world Interweb and read what I wrote, that would be delightful. I thought my daddy, my sister, and my brother might be interested—maybe even a few friends from college. I knew from the get-go that my mama wouldn't touch the blog with a ten-foot pole since she often reminds us that she doesn't even know how to turn on the e-mail, but I was okay with that.

For about six years I kept up my regular routine of blogging in between piling up clean clothes on the guest room bed, finding new and inventive ways to incorporate bacon into our meals, and watching more than my fair share of Bravo after our little boy was asleep.

I know that last thing probably sounds super shallow.

That's because it is.

But sometimes, after a long, hard day, I need to hear Ramona on *The Real Housewives of New York City* say that she'd wear a certain item of clothing "in a heartflash."

It comforts me.

Then one day in April 2011, I was folding clothes from the aforementioned guest room pile when an expression that Papaw Davis used all the time came to mind: *I think I need a little salty to cut the sweet.* He'd say it as he pushed back from the table after devouring a helping of Mamaw Davis's homemade blueberry cobbler, and it was always a signal that he might need one more piece of fried chicken to balance out his sugar intake. I don't know about y'all, but that tendency to temper an overly jellied biscuit with one last piece of thick-sliced bacon or to alleviate the effects of too much homemade banana pudding with a sliver of beef tenderloin is at least one family member's story at every holiday gathering. And as I stacked folded towel on top of folded towel that afternoon, I thought about how that expression applies to more than just food.

For the first time in my life, there was a book I wanted to write. And it blows my mind just a little bit that you're about to read it.

Mamaw and Papaw Davis didn't live to see me graduate from high school; honestly, I have no idea if either of them knew how much I liked to write. But make no mistake: their example and their legacy are precisely why I treasure our family stories and why I feel privileged to share them. They couldn't have known how deeply I was soaking in the words and the expressions and the testimonies and the laughter that surrounded me when I would perch on the edge of a breakfast room chair and listen to the grown-ups hold court. But I was taking it all in—and I've never forgotten.

So that's all a very long-winded way of saying that, for me, this book is my twenty-first-century version of Mamaw and Papaw Davis's kitchen. I haven't really figured out a way to serve you some of Mamaw's sweet tea and apple tarts while you read, much less her homemade chocolate pie, which could make even the staunchest Episcopalian lift up holy hands and offer the Lord spontaneous songs of praise and thanksgiving.

But the welcome mat is out, the crazy is on full display, and there's always room for one more around our table.

I hope you'll feel right at home.

CHAPTER ONE

Not to Mention That Her Apple Tarts Would Change Your Whole Life

So, I HAVE A THEORY.

It's not a theory about science or religion or politics. Oh, heavens, no. That would be a complete departure from the very fiber of my personality.

But I do have a theory about memory. More specifically, I have a theory about how we remember people.

Are you ready?

Prepare to be underwhelmed, my friends.

My theory is that we typically have one dominant "fallback" memory that becomes our go-to mental image when we think about somebody.

Now that I've typed that out, by the way, I'm thinking that maybe it's not so much a *theory* as a loose, unverifiable observation.

But let's just run with it. Because whenever I think about Papaw Sims, for example, I picture him leaning over his deep freeze and asking if I'd rather have chocolate, vanilla, or strawberry ice cream. Whenever I think about Uncle Joe, I picture him dozing in his recliner with a stack of paperwork on his lap—and a ten-key adding machine within arm's reach. And whenever I think about Mamaw Davis, my maternal grandmother, I picture her looking over her shoulder and grinning while she's standing at the stove. Maybe even scooping a little Crisco out of the can.

The mental picture of Mamaw standing at the stove is one of the most enduring images of my childhood, mainly because she stood at that stove so faithfully. She cooked three hot meals a day, seven days a week. There was never anything made from a box, either—no powdery macaroni and cheese or Hamburger Helper. Oh, no, ma'am. There was hot cornbread, beef stroganoff over rice, pot roast with carrots and potatoes, fried chicken, creamed potatoes, fresh peas, fried squash, fried okra (I have to pause for a moment whenever I mention Mamaw's fried okra and give it the reverence and honor that it is due), egg custard pie, pound cake—I could go on and on.

We didn't have all that food at one time, mind you, or else we'd have alternated trips to Mamaw's table with trips to the cardiac care unit, but there was always something delicious and homemade on that stove. Mamaw didn't think she was doing anything special—she was just taking care of her family the best way she knew how—but I think her children and grandchildren can all testify to the fact that those meals she cooked ministered to us like a good Sunday sermon. And she didn't have to say a single word.

For at least one week a summer—sometimes more—my mama and my daddy, along with my aunt Choxie, who is Mama's sister, and Chox's husband, my uncle Joe, would ship my cousin Paige and me off to Mamaw and Papaw Davis's pretty white farmhouse in Moss Rose, Mississippi—about thirty minutes from my hometown of Myrtlewood. Since Paige would have been born in the early 1900s if she'd had any say in the matter, she thrived on Mamaw and Papaw's farm. She was perfectly content to pick blackberries, walk through the chicken coops, amble about in the pastures, and count cows. I, on the other hand, was a total scaredy-cat, wary of tall grass that made me itch and bumblebees that refused to be swatted away.

I had issues when I was indoors, too. When Paige and I would go to bed at night, exhausted from our day's adventures, I'd usually make it ten or fifteen minutes before I'd sprint down the hall and crawl into bed with Mamaw and Papaw. Every floorboard creak sounded to me like imminent danger, so I settled into sleep much more easily underneath the cool hum of the AC window unit in my grandparents' room. No way could the boogeyman get me in there. Not on Papaw's watch. He was broad shouldered, barrel chested, and utterly devoted to his family—a security blanket in human form.

Papaw had some health problems when I was ten, and not too long afterward he and Mamaw decided to downsize and find a smaller house with a lot less land. Somebody later told my mama that Papaw was thinking ahead—he was worried something would happen to him and Mamaw would be stuck with the responsibilities of the farm. On top of that, he didn't want her to be living in a relatively remote area all by herself. So they sold the farmhouse (and the farm) and moved to a blond brick house that was just catty-corner from Moss Rose's Methodist church.

Papaw added a den to the back of the new-to-them house so there would be a nice big gathering place for the family, and when we had our first Sunday lunch there a month or so after they moved in, Mamaw stood at her new stove and carried out the ministry of the homemade chicken pie just like she'd always done. Paige and I missed the backyard of the old house and the pipe swing with the eight-foot chain that hung from the branches of an old oak tree, but there was a barn to explore and plenty of room to roam. That was all we needed.

The following winter Mama and Chox hosted a tea at Mamaw and Papaw's house to celebrate their fiftieth wedding anniversary. Mama and Choxie's brother, Bill, who lived three hours away, was there too, and in my opinion Bill's presence always elevated a family gathering a couple of notches. He drove a sports car, reminded me of Burt Reynolds, and delivered one-liners better than anybody else I knew. If that weren't enough, Mama and Chox let Paige and me serve the punch, and we were certain such a grown-up responsibility meant we'd hit the big time. Papaw wore his nicest suit, and Mamaw wore a pretty dress that she'd made for the occasion, along with a corsage that Sister had bought for her at a florist's shop in Myrtlewood. They made an adorable couple.

Papaw's personality came alive in a big group of folks, so he was in his element that afternoon. Mamaw, on the other hand, was much more introverted and soft spoken. Every once in a while Papaw would put his hand on her back and whisper, "You doing okay, Lucy?"

She'd grin and say, "I'm fine, John."

But even at eleven years old I knew it was hard for her to be the center of attention. Her sweet, servant spirit shone just fine without the aid of any limelight, and part of me wondered if she wasn't going to sneak out of her own anniversary party so she could get in the kitchen and make everybody some chicken and dumplings. She hung in there with the socializing, though, and she stood by Papaw's side until the front door closed and Mama and Chox practically raced to see who could be the first one to take off her high-heeled shoes.

What none of us knew at the time, though, was how much Mamaw was struggling with her health. Then again, not even *she* knew how sick she was. Having been plagued by a general feeling of weakness as well as liver problems during the past several years, she initially thought that she was dealing with more of the same. Over the next few months, however, she and Papaw traveled to Myrtlewood almost weekly for doctor's visits, and early that fall—about eight months after their fiftieth anniversary—Papaw told the family that the doctor had confirmed their worst fear: cancer. Other than helping Mamaw manage her pain and keeping her as comfortable as possible, there wasn't much the doctors could do.

Mamaw was admitted to the hospital in Myrtlewood right before Thanksgiving, and for the next two weeks Mama, Chox, and Papaw rarely left her side. Mama would pick up Paige and me from school—we were fourteen and twelve at that point— and we'd do our homework in the waiting room down the hall from Mamaw's room while we drank Cokes and ate Dolly Madison fruit pies from the vending machine. Mama or Chox would take us downstairs to the hospital cafeteria for supper, and we'd eventually go home whenever they felt Mamaw was settled for the night. It broke their hearts to see her in pain, and they took their role as her advocates very seriously. It wasn't quite like Shirley MacLaine at the nurses' station in *Terms of Endearment*— Mama and Chox were far too polite to make a scene—but in their own Southern ways, they didn't mess around.

By mid-December the weather had turned windy and cold, and Mamaw showed no signs of getting better. One Tuesday night Papaw needed to drive back to Moss Rose to get a change of clothes and a few other things, and since Mama and Chox didn't want him to stay at the house by himself, they suggested that he take Paige and me with him. We had school the next day, but they were far more worried about Papaw than about our missing an hour of social studies. So off we went.

The ride to Moss Rose in Papaw's Oldsmobile 88 was a quiet one, and by the time we arrived at Mamaw and Papaw's house, we were all pretty worn out. It was the first time I'd walked through their back door without immediately seeing Mamaw standing at the stove, and while we didn't stop and take time to vocalize our feelings or anything like that, I think it's safe to say that we all felt her absence.

Paige and I brushed our teeth in silence that night, standing in the guest bath that always smelled like a combination of rubbing alcohol and Mercurochrome. We walked down the hall to tell Papaw good-night and found him lying on top of the bed-spread, staring at the ceiling with his arms crossed over his chest. Paige and I sat down beside him, not really knowing what to say. Papaw spoke up first and uttered six words that have stayed with me for more than thirty years.

"She was mighty sweet, wasn't she?"

It struck me as strange that he used the past tense, but Paige and I certainly didn't correct him. We tried our best to comfort him as his shoulders began to shake and the tears started to fall. And while I don't have any idea what time it was when Paige and I finally fell asleep, I do know that Papaw's quiet sobs were the last sound either of us heard.

Early the next morning, around five o'clock, there was a knock on the door. Mama, Daddy, Chox, and Joe had come to tell us what Papaw's heart had told him the night before.

Up to that point in my life—and I was every bit of twelve

years old—I'd been all about ballet lessons, my snazzy new Merlin game, *American Top 40*, and Nancy Drew mysteries. So for me, Mamaw's death was my first glimpse into what family life looks like in the midst of sadness and grief and heartache. I couldn't have put words to it at the time, I don't think, but somehow I could sense that there was beauty in all that brokenness, that there were little patches of light that permeated the darkness. Yes, there was sorrow and pain—but there was also love and comfort and laughter and joy. There was a confidence that something bigger was at work, an assurance of "an eternal glory that far outweighs them all" (2 Corinthians 4:17, NIV).

So while Mamaw's death certainly isn't my happiest memory, I can honestly say that it will forever be one that I treasure. Because that memory, by God's grace, continues to teach me.

And even now, more than three decades later, I hold that memory in my heart real tight.

And I watch.

And I listen.

CHAPTER TWO

When the Biggest Portion of All Is the Love

OVER THE LAST SEVERAL YEARS my hometown of Myrtlewood, Mississippi, has enjoyed a little bit of a building boom. A new mall at the edge of town spurred all sorts of development in the surrounding area, and what was once a commercial no-man's-land is now a bustling shopping hub for four or five counties. Compared to when I was growing up, Myrtlewood has become very hip and with it and now. And also fancy.

A sure sign that it was the dawn of a new retail day was the arrival of three popular chain restaurants: Olive Garden, Red Lobster, and Outback Steakhouse, which my mother-in-law, Martha, likes to refer to as "the Outbacks." Martha, who's every bit of five feet tall and wears a size next-to-nothing in her beloved three-quarter-sleeve jackets, enjoys the occasional trip to the Outbacks. She thinks their food is out of this world, but the portions throw her for a little bit of a loop. After all, she is a person who is absolutely stuffed after a lunch of half a ham sandwich and two Pringles, so it's understandable that she feels a smidge overwhelmed by a plate of Alice Springs Chicken. Especially since it's, you know, the size of her head.

As a person who grew up in a family whose attitude about food was "If a little bit is good, then more is so much better," I've always been somewhat mystified by Martha's aversion to a big ole plate of, well, *anything*. However, when I was about twenty-eight, I realized that Martha's disdain for large portions was the real dadgum deal. At the time, my husband and I were newlyweds, and Martha and her mother—an equally petite woman named Lelia, who was affectionately known as Sissie to her family and most of her friends—came for a visit. David and I were living in South Louisiana, and we were excited about having company for the weekend and eager to take them to a few of our favorite restaurants. Granted, Martha and Sissie each weighed every bit of a hundred pounds soaking wet and weren't exactly known for putting away the food. (However, woe be unto you if you tried to get between Martha and a slice of really good wedding cake— she'd stab you between the knuckles with a dessert fork before she'd share even the tiniest bite.) Even so, we thought they'd enjoy a little bit of Cajun culinary flava.

Because Martha and Sissie, as I'm sure you can imagine, were all about the flava.

So that Saturday we took them to lunch at a restaurant close to our house. Once we were settled at our table and had talked our way through all the menu options, Martha and Sissie ordered some kind of chicken plate, David ordered a hamburger, and I ordered a big salad with fried chicken on it.

(Because do you know what makes lettuce better?)

(Listen, and I will tell you.)

(FRIED MEAT.)

('Tis true.)

Our food arrived not too long after we ordered, and as soon as Martha saw everyone's plates, she couldn't contain herself.

"Sophie! My word! Have you ever seen such portions? I've never in my life seen such portions! I can't imagine who could eat these portions! I mean, Sissie and I—well, we just don't eat like this. I mean, sometimes we might split a hamburger from the Wendy's or maybe order a snack pack from Kentucky Fried Chicken, but my word! These portions! I've just never seen such!"

I wanted to take it all in stride. I really did. But the truth of the matter is that I was borderline offended. I understood where she was coming from, and Lord knows I had loved her and Sissie to pieces since I was a child in Myrtlewood and our families sat on neighboring pews during the 10:55 service at Mission Hill United Methodist Church. That being said, I still wasn't in the mood to sit there and feel self-conscious about the size of my salad just because I happened to be eating lunch with two precious women who typically felt full and completely satisfied after they'd eaten a tablespoon of potato casserole and four English peas.

And that's why, a few seconds later, when Martha wrapped up her mealtime observations with one final chorus of "Who could possibly eat these portions?" I responded the only way I knew how. I grabbed my fork with renewed determination and cheerfully replied, "Your daughter-in-law can!" And then I stuffed approximately a fourth of my salad into my mouth on pure principle.

Oh, I could do more than just eat those portions, mind you. I COULD EAT THEM WITH AUTHORITY.

Given our experience at lunch that day—and, if I'm honest, at every restaurant we visited over the next ten years—I wasn't really surprised by Martha's reaction to the Outbacks once it made its debut in my hometown. It was so much food, just so much food! You've never seen such food! And even if Martha and her friend Rubena, who was her favorite buddy when it came to all things shopping and dining, went to the Outbacks and split something (even if they split something!), it was still just way more food than they could possibly eat. I mean, there was just no way they could eat those portions!

HAVE YOU SEEN THOSE PORTIONS?

Besides, if Martha had to pick a steakhouse that was going to be the subject of her undying devotion, there's no question that the winner was situated about a quarter of a mile away, just up the road and on the other side of the highway.

The Western Sizzlin.

Truth be told, I can relate to Martha's fondness for the Western Sizzlin. As a matter of fact, I have Sizzlin-related memories that go back to my childhood. When I was growing up, our family didn't eat out very much, mainly because there weren't a whole lot of places to go. Combine that with the fact that my daddy is perhaps the most frugal man alive (and when I say *frugal*, what I really mean is cheap, but I don't mean that as an insult, and OH, BELIEVE ME, my daddy wouldn't take it as one), and the end result was a family that ate out maybe two or three times a year.

On those rare occasions when we did eat out, we'd always go to a steakhouse, and back then the two options were Bonanza and—you guessed it—Western Sizzlin. I usually voted for Bonanza because I liked to visit the salad bar and fill up my bowl with bacon bits, croutons, and Thousand Island dressing. Perhaps that's where I first developed my sophisticated culinary taste—I'll ponder that possibility the next time that I find myself dipping Ritz crackers into a jar of peanut butter and then washing them down with an ice-cold can of Diet Mountain Dew.

Bonanza closed about twenty-five years ago, but Western Sizzlin is still alive and, well, sizzlin'. Martha is one of their most loyal diners, and I think the main reason for that is because the employees there have always been incredibly kind to her. For years Martha drove Rubena to the Western Sizzlin on Thursday nights, and they always ordered the same thing: the petite sirloin with a baked potato, and peach cobbler for dessert. According to Martha, if you don't time it just right, the Western Sizzlin might not have enough peaches in their cobbler (she doesn't mean to complain! she wouldn't want to complain! and it's still delicious!), but the portion sizes are absolutely perfect.

That is some high praise, my friends.

Martha and Rubena's bond went far deeper than those weekly trips to Western Sizzlin, though. They had been childhood friends in Myrtlewood and forged a friendship that carried them through all the stages of their lives. They played dolls when they were little girls, navigated high school together as teenagers, and shared the journey of raising children and taking care of their families as adults. Since Martha grew up Methodist and Rubena grew up Baptist, they didn't go to the same church, but they loved to visit the fifty-plus luncheons at each other's churches whenever they could. Their devotion to one another has always been inspiring— to this day, I've never heard Martha say an unkind word about Rubena, and I strongly suspect that the reverse is also true.

About fifteen years ago Rubena was diagnosed with macular degeneration, a disease that causes a gradual loss of peripheral vision, but Martha and Rubena both took the vision-related changes in stride. Martha would hold Rubena's elbow as they walked through "the Dillards," and whenever they'd split up to look at dresses (Martha had to look in the petites' section! the petites' section! otherwise she'd spend a small fortune in alterations trying to get the shoulder seams moved! so she shopped in the petites' section!), Rubena would inevitably call for Martha to come read a price tag or a brand name or the fine print at the bottom of a coupon.

They'd usually shop for an hour or so, then leave the Dillards with one or two new things each: a skirt for Rubena, a jacket for Martha, some cute clip-on earrings to match that blouse Martha had found in the Goody's a few years ago—you know, the one she thought would be perfectly wonderful with her black slacks, only they didn't have the blouse in her size? So she got the manager named Kevin to call another store and the other store had it in her size so the next time she was in Piney Bend with her friend Mary Ann they stopped and picked it up? Only now, do you know— DO YOU KNOW—that the Myrtlewood Goody's is closed and she worries sometimes about the manager named Kevin? And how he's doing and if his family is well? Not to mention the fact that you can hardly find those Alfred Dunner separates now that the Goody's is closed, you really can't! you just can't! oh, no, you can't!

Sorry. Apparently I was overtaken by a Martha Moment.

If you ever have the privilege of meeting Martha, you will find that you start to experience Martha Moments within thirty to forty-five seconds of the introduction.

These Martha Moments, they are contagious.

Over a period of several years Rubena's eyes continued to get worse, but the girls' shopping trips didn't stop. "The girls," by the way, is how Martha refers to her friends, who range in age from seventy to eighty-five. And let me tell you what: the girls are absolutely darlin'.

There's no telling how many miles Rubena and Martha walked

in that mall over the years—with Martha holding Rubena's elbow all the while—and Martha always liked to recount their latest shopping finds whenever I was in town and would stop by her house for a visit. I never knew what to expect when Martha would launch into the tale of their latest adventure at the Tulip Creek Mall, but one of the most memorable was the long, involved saga of trying to find a housecoat for Rubena at Belk. Or, as Martha calls it, "the Belks."

The housecoat story was an epic tale involving crowded sale racks, charmingly uninformed clerks, and unattractive housecoat patterns. Martha relayed the details with such passion—and was so insistent about Rubena's desperate need for a housecoat—that I started to feel like I must have missed a critical piece of information that would explain the urgency. So about fifteen minutes into the story, I stopped Martha to try to clarify.

"Hold on," I said. "I think I missed something. Why exactly were y'all looking for a housecoat for Rubena? Was she getting ready to go out of town? Or go to the hospital?"

"No, nothing like that!" she exclaimed. "She just needed a new one! She needed a new one! Because, well, she still likes to cook her breakfast every morning, and she cooks breakfast in her housecoat, but, you know, she can't see very well!"

"Okay," I replied, still feeling a little clueless.

"Well, she gets in front of her stove and can't really see what she's doing and she has just scorched her housecoat sleeves to pieces! Just scorched 'em to pieces!"

I sat perfectly still for a moment, unsure of how to respond, but after a few seconds I decided it never hurts to go with sincerity.

"Well," I responded, "I surely do hope y'all found one. Sounds like Rubena really needed that new housecoat."

"Oh, she did," Martha answered. "And there was a darlin'

one on the sale rack. It was perfectly adorable. PERFECTLY ADORABLE. But I never could get a price for it. COULD NOT get a price. For all I know, it's still there, still just hanging there, and you'd think that the Belks would like to sell it, wouldn't you? I guess they just didn't want to sell it! At least not to us!"

Not too long after that—less than a year after the Unfortunate Housecoat Incident, as my husband and I refer to it—Martha called to tell us that Rubena had been diagnosed with an aggressive form of cancer. It was the first time in my married life when I could remember hearing sadness in Martha's voice. Oh, she remained upbeat and positive and unfailingly cheerful when she and Rubena were together, but make no mistake: she was absolutely devastated. On top of the other challenges of the last few years—taking care of her mother, dealing with Sissie's accompanying health concerns, eventually coming to terms with the fact that Sissie needed to be in a nursing home—the news of her lifelong best friend's terminal illness hit Martha hard. Whenever we talked and I asked Martha how she was handling it all, she always responded the same way:

"It's a lot, Sophie. It's just a lot."

And it was.

Martha and Rubena continued to get out and about as much as they could, and once a week or so, if Rubena felt up to it, Martha would still drive them to the Western Sizzlin. It was their little tradition. All the waiters and waitresses knew them by name—so did the cooks in the kitchen, for that matter—and they always made sure "Miss Martha" and "Miss Rubena" had plenty of sweet tea with their meals and plenty of coffee with their desserts. From time to time the young girl who worked at the cash register would even wrap a hot cinnamon roll in a napkin for Martha and hand it to her after she'd paid for her meal.

Martha always tried to press an extra dollar or two into the girl's hand, but she wouldn't take it.

"It's just for you, Miss Martha," the cashier would say. "We know how much you love our cinnamon rolls."

I don't know if that sweet girl had any idea how Martha's heart was breaking as she watched her oldest and dearest friend battle cancer. But I can promise you that, in the simplest and most profound way, those cinnamon rolls meant the world to Martha. They really did.

The shopping trips and dinner trips slowed down as Rubena's condition worsened. And about six months after she received her diagnosis, Rubena went to be with Jesus. She was like a sister to Martha until the very end.

Martha would tell you even now that she would have never wanted her dear friend to suffer, that it makes her smile to think of Rubena in heaven. She would tell you how grateful she is for the blessing of having a lifelong friend who, for the better part of seventy years, had been a supportive, encouraging example of Christlike love.

But she would also tell you that she misses her friend every single day, that she feels lonely sometimes when she goes to the Belks and doesn't have to run over to the dresses section to check a size for Rubena. And she would tell you that she'd give anything if they could leave the mall together and eat dinner at the Western Sizzlin just one more time.

A couple of years ago I was sitting at the bar in Martha's kitchen, eating a piece of caramel cake while Martha was on the phone making supper plans with a friend. When she hung up, Martha walked over to where I was sitting, and she had a smile as wide as Texas on her face.

"Well," she said, "that was Mary Ann. I think some of the girls and I are going to eat supper at the Western Sizzlin tomorrow night."

"Oh, really?" I asked, pushing away my plate and wondering if it would just smack of irony if I asked Martha for a post–caramel cake Diet Coke.

"Yes! We are!" Martha answered. "You know how I love their petite sirloin. And sometimes after I visit Mother at the nursing home, I like to swing by the Western Sizzlin and pick up a to-go plate and bring it back here. And do you know that darlin' cashier still wraps up a cinnamon roll and gives it to me? I try to pay! I really do try to pay! But she always says, 'Miss Martha, I know how you love them, and I know . . .'"

Martha's voice trailed off at the end of her sentence. I didn't really understand why, so as I opened the cabinet to grab a glass, I said, "What? She knows what?"

Martha cleared her throat. "'I know how you miss your friend,' she says. She says, 'Miss Martha, I know how you miss your friend.'"

We sat in silence for a second, and I wondered what that would feel like. I thought about Emma Kate and Marion and Daphne and the rest of my friends—friends who have been a part of my life for so long—and I thought about how hard it would be to lose them.

"But," Martha piped up, "tomorrow night I'll go with the girls. It'll be so much fun! Just more fun! And I know that some of them would rather eat at the Outbacks, but I do like the Western Sizzlin. You know how I like it there! Their portions are absolutely perfect! Oh, I surely do like it there."

Then she grinned and said, "They don't always have enough peaches in their cobbler, though."

But don't tell anyone that she said that.

CHAPTER THREE

When the Fine China Is, Um, Refining

WHEN MAMA AND DADDY got engaged, Mama selected Rosenthal's Hillside as their fine china pattern. Even now Sister and I talk about how absolutely stunning it is. The plates are creamy white, rimmed in gold, with small yellow, light pink, and purple flowers circling a delicate hot-pink rose in the center. It's timeless, elegant, and every bit as beautiful as it was when Mama picked it out in January 1954.

For the first ten years of Mama and Daddy's marriage, Mama used her Rosenthal Hillside to set a fabulous table. She's always loved to entertain, and I can only imagine the dinner parties she and Daddy had with the Chandlers, the Guys, the Waltons, and the Murrells, among others. They no doubt had a ball as they ate and laughed and carried on, and I can just picture Mama, at the end of one of her delicious meals, serving coffee with her Hillside cups and saucers while the ladies nibbled at homemade strawberry shortcake and the men moved to the chairs in the living room so they could comfortably solve the world's problems.

In the mid '60s Mama and Daddy built a house out in the country, about eight miles from town, and though the area is well populated now, it was the middle of nowhere back then. The house sat off the road on about twelve acres, and it was a perfect place to enjoy a little breathing room and raise their two children. (Since I'm ten years younger than my closest sibling, I wasn't even a blip on their radar back then.)

Mama took great care getting her Rosenthal ready for the move, taking extra time to wrap each cup and saucer in layer upon layer of tissue paper so it wouldn't rattle or break after she put the box in her car. Mama's packing skills are legendary and the subject of equal measures of amusement and reverence in our family. When Mama wrapped up my own fine china when my husband, son, and I moved into our current house, the coffee cups were so elaborately bound that I needed an X-ACTO knife to release them from their packing-tape prison. I certainly wasn't surprised; when I was in college, there were a few times when Mama sent a care package I was certain I'd never be able to open. I just didn't possess those levels of superhuman strength.

Seriously. It's not a package from my mama unless you break a sweat trying to get into it.

So even though I wasn't alive when Mama meticulously packed her Rosenthal for the big move to the country, there's not a doubt in my mind that she had every intention of handling those dishes with the utmost care. It wouldn't surprise me a bit if she'd planned to gingerly place the box on the front seat of her car and secure it with the seat belt.

Precious cargo, you understand.

Well, at some point during the move, Daddy filled the back

of his truck with boxes so he could take them to the new house. He and Uncle Bill were handling most of the moving duties, and anything that was fragile was supposed to go in Mama's car. All the durable, sturdy stuff got thrown in the back of the truck.

Unfortunately, though, what neither Mama nor Daddy realized was that an errant box—one that was full of Mama's beloved Rosenthal Hillside cups and saucers—had gotten mixed in with the boxes of kitchen utensils and decorative pillows and garden tools in the back of Daddy's truck. That carefully packed china was no match for an old truck and a bumpy dirt road, and you'd better believe that when Mama eventually realized how her prized porcelain had traveled to the new house, she made a beeline for the box. As soon as she began to unpack it, she discovered that those cups and saucers were nothing more than chips and shards.

Now, I've never known my mama to harbor unforgiveness toward anyone, but the accidental destruction of all that gorgeous Rosenthal china was a sanctifying experience for her. Mama has always found comfort in Scripture, and I daresay that if she hadn't trusted so deeply in the book of James's admonition to "count it all joy, my brothers, when you meet trials of various kinds," those broken cups and saucers might have caused a permanent rift in her marriage, as well as a touch of the post-traumatic stress disorder.

And to be perfectly honest, I think Mama may have struggled for a day or two with the end of that verse, which assures us that our trials ultimately mold us into people who are "perfect and complete, lacking in nothing."

Because GUESS WHAT, JAMES? SHE WAS STILL LACKING THOSE ROSENTHAL CUPS AND SAUCERS.

Clearly James wasn't privy to the details of Mama's harrowing china ordeal when he wrote his epistle.

Naturally, Mama recovered. Laughed about it, even. She contented herself with her remaining Rosenthal Hillside salad and dinner plates, and I'll have you know that she still uses them, almost fifty years later.

The Lord always leaves a remnant, you know.

I'm pretty sure that James would agree.

CHAPTER FOUR

The Saga of the Homemade Biscuits

MY DADDY HAS NEVER been big on cooking. In fact, my sister and brother and I have always said that if, heaven forbid, something should happen to Mama, Daddy will have to remarry or else he'll starve. I hope that doesn't sound harsh, because I really don't mean it that way. It's just that while some men enjoy getting in the kitchen and spreading their culinary wings, my daddy is not one of them. He much prefers to spread his culinary wings while sitting at the dining room table and enjoying the food that my mama has lovingly prepared for him.

And for the record, Mama has lovingly prepared that food for him for almost sixty years. The math involved in that level of cooking dedication blows my mind, because three hot meals a day times 350 days a year (I'm allowing for some days off for travel and such) times sixty years equals roughly 63,000 meals, at which point you have to conclude that it might be appropriate at this stage in Mama's life for somebody to give her a bottomless gift card to the Cracker Barrel.

In all fairness, though, I should mention that Daddy has been known to pitch in with the cooking duties from time to time, like when he would help Mama shell peas from the garden or man the grill when we were having company. When I was in junior high, he even decided that he was going to learn to make biscuits—a topic that is still so sensitive with Mama that I'm almost afraid to mention it. Since we're coming up on almost thirty years since the event, though, I'm going to throw caution to the wind and tell you about it.

For many years my daddy worked faithfully as the Cooperative Extension agent in my hometown. Since his job required him to spend a good bit of time traveling from one end of the county to the other, advising local farmers and gardeners about their crops and lawns and soil and what-have-you, he frequently benefited from the generosity of some wonderful Southern cooks. More often than not, he'd come home with a batch of squash pickles from a lady who lived in a nearby community or a Tupperware container full of chow-chow from a man who farmed near the state line or a mason jar of plum jelly from a widowed woman out at the reservoir. Now that I'm older, I can recognize those homemade delicacies as flat-out treasures, and today I'd pay cash money for a small sample of any of them. But when I was growing up, I really didn't understand why some homemade strawberry preserves from Mrs. Nicholson, our faithful church pianist, were such a big deal to Mama and Daddy.

Youth is wasted on the young, I'm afraid.

On more than one occasion Daddy told us that there was an older lady—we'll call her Mrs. Cunningham—from Myrtlewood whose homemade biscuits were nothing short of legendary, and after Daddy spoke at Mrs. Cunningham's Community Development Club meeting one day and sampled those biscuits, he sort of offhandedly mentioned to her that he'd love to know how to make them. In retrospect, the very notion that Daddy showed any interest in knowing how to make biscuits strikes me as a clear indication that he must have been in the throes of a midlife crisis, only instead of going the stereotypical midlife crisis route and buying a convertible, he went the country boy route and figured he'd learn to whip up a Southern mealtime staple.

It was totally uncharacteristic behavior on his part. That's all I'm saying.

Anyway, Daddy and Mrs. Cunningham set up a time for her to show him how to make those biscuits, and Daddy never said anything about the biscuit-making tutorial to Mama because quite frankly he couldn't fathom that she'd care. Mama has always been super laid back about Daddy's work and golf and sports interests—she just doesn't put a whole lot of demands on his time (which, by the way, is part of the reason her two daughters tend to err on the side of fiercely independent)—so it probably didn't occur to Daddy to bring Mama in the biscuit loop.

Well.

I still don't know the exact chain of events, but somehow a reporter from *The Myrtlewood Tribune* found out that Daddy had asked Mrs. Cunningham to show him how to make biscuits. The reporter thought it might be fun to document the cooking lesson for the paper, so she tagged along when Daddy learned how to fix those storied biscuits. About a week later—on a Wednesday, I believe—the lead story on the front page of the "People" section was how Mrs. Cunningham shared her biscuit-making secrets with the local Cooperative Extension agent (that would be Daddy). There was an assortment of pictures, too—Daddy rolling out the dough, Daddy listening attentively to Mrs. Cunningham, Daddy admiring a cast-iron skillet filled with tall, fluffy biscuits. It was a delightful article.

Or so I thought.

For all my life, you see, my mama has been a gracious, even-tempered lady. From my perspective, at least, she's been in the same mood for the better part of forty years.

(Whereas I have a tendency to get a little worked up and stressed out and high strung from time to time.)

(And when I say "from time to time," of course, what I mean is "on a daily basis.")

My mama, on the other hand, is calm, patient, and steady. I'm sure the daily rigors of motherhood frustrated her every once in a while, but she rarely showed it. As a matter of fact, the only time I can remember her raising her voice for more than a few seconds was when I was nine and served as an acolyte in church with my cousin Paige. After Paige and I fulfilled our candle-lighting responsibilities, we took our seats in the center of the front pew and proceeded to practice our limited sign language skills for the remainder of the service. Since Paige and I didn't know any signs for words, we spelled out everything letter by letter.

D-O Y-O-U W-A-N-T T-O G-O S-W-I-M-M-I-N-G A-F-T-E-R C-H-U-R-C-H?

N-O. I T-H-I-N-K W-E S-H-O-U-L-D W-A-L-K T-O J-I-T-N-E-Y J-U-N-I-O-R A-N-D G-E-T I-C-E-E-S!

O-K. D-I-D Y-O-U S-E-E S-C-O-T-T B-A-I-O O-N T-V L-A-S-T N-I-G-H-T?

Oh, we were just as tickled as we could be by our resourcefulness because, you see, *technically* we weren't talking in church. To our eleven- and nine-year-old selves, that was the genius part of the whole sign language plan. Mama and my aunt Choxie, however, were none too pleased with our failure to respond to the icy glares they were sending our way from the choir loft, and within about thirty minutes of that afternoon's Sunday lunch, I'd gained two valuable bits of insight: (1) not only could my mama raise her voice, she could raise it *effectively* while swatting my rear end with a Bolo paddle, and (2) if I ever had any intention of waving my hands around in church like that again, it had better be the result of a fresh move of the Holy Spirit.

And let's be honest. We were members of a conservative Methodist church where people cut their eyes and stared if someone said, "Amen!" during the preacher's sermon. So even if there had been a fresh move of the Holy Spirit that caused me to wave my hands, the expected response would be, "Quench it, sister, and be reverent."

JOHN WESLEY WOULD WANT IT THAT WAY.

All that to say, Sign Language Sunday taught me that Mama definitely had the capacity for some righteous indignation, and several years later I got another glimpse of it when she opened her copy of *The Myrtlewood Tribune* and saw the article about Daddy learning to make biscuits with Mrs. Cunningham. I'd never really understood the expression "It made her blood run cold," but that Wednesday I witnessed it. As Mama read all about Daddy's Great Big Biscuit Adventure, the color drained from her face, and her lips tightened in a look of utter indignation.

"Well," she remarked in a low, level tone as she slowly folded up the newspaper and set it on the kitchen counter, "I have never. I have NEVER."

I was an oblivious teenager at the time, so I had no idea why she was upset. I was also too young to pry too deeply into my mama's business, so I tried not to cross any parent/child boundaries when I said, "Mama? You okay?"

"Oh, I'm fine," she answered. But those pursed lips told another story.

Later that afternoon I was able to piece together the problem when I overheard/eavesdropped on a phone conversation between Mama and Chox. Mama was as indignant as I'd ever heard her.

"The thing is, Chox," she began, "I resent it. I resent the whole thing, to tell you the truth. I mean, what am I supposed to say to people when I go to the Winn-Dixie? How am I supposed to respond?"

I still wasn't sure why Mama was so upset. Since Mrs. Cunningham was the kindest, most grandmotherly woman you ever did see—and since Mama thought the world of her—I knew Mrs. Cunningham wasn't the problem. But given Mama's level of uncharacteristic exasperation, there had to be more to the story. My brain grappled with all sorts of possibilities. Maybe Mama didn't think the story was newsworthy. Maybe she was aggravated that Daddy hadn't told her about the article. Or maybe she didn't like the clothes Daddy was wearing in the pictures.

That last option wasn't all that unlikely, really. Mama was forever trying to get Daddy to be more mindful about his wardrobe selections, but Daddy never had the slightest interest in the latest styles or trends. Mama always contended that since Daddy's job required him to be on television a few times a month, it might not be a bad idea for him to invest in a few nice-looking shirts and sweaters. But Daddy was perfectly content with whatever was clean, provided it was free of any gaping holes.

❧

It was actually about the same time as the biscuit fiasco when Mama's frustration with Daddy's clothing choices came to a head.

One night Mama and I were watching the local news while a reporter interviewed Daddy about something like tomato plants or Japanese beetles or soil erosion, which is such a coincidence since I considered writing this book about those exact same topics. Anyway, Mama commented that Daddy was wearing his favorite sweater—a remark that was made with some degree of disapproval in light of Mama and Daddy's ongoing discussions regarding the merits of brand-name clothing vs. off brands. Mama stood firmly on the side of buying brand names, arguing that it just made good sense to pay a little extra for better quality. Daddy contended that all clothing came off the same assembly line and the only differences were the emblems and labels someone plastered on the shirts or pants or sweaters before they left the factory.

(I believe we've just pinpointed why I like to shop at Stein Mart.)

(Stein Mart has brand names at discount prices, which means I satisfy both sides of my gene pool *at the exact same time*.)

(What can I say? I'm a people pleaser.)

(If that's okay with you, of course.)

So.

As Mama and I watched the interview, she acknowledged that Daddy was doing a great job even though his clothing selection, in her opinion, left something to be desired. And several moments later, she noticed an unexpected sweater complication: the fox that signified that This Sweater Is a Fine Utilitarian Garment from JCPenney seemed slightly askew. Sort of like the fox decided to make a run for it and, as he attempted his escape, accidentally caught his back left leg in a loose thread.

As any good Southern woman worth her smelling salts would do, Mama immediately decided she had to rectify the situation.

When Daddy got home later that night and changed his clothes, Mama picked up the sweater and carefully removed the injured fox, only to find a hole behind it. There was talk of trying to reattach the fox, but since one of his back legs was past the point of rehabilitation, we had to put him down.

Life in the animal kingdom can be brutal, y'all.

Most people would've probably thrown away the sweater, but my mama is a child of the Depression and therefore doesn't throw anything away until she is completely and utterly convinced that the item in question can't be repurposed in any way whatsoever. No kidding—when Mama and Daddy moved a few summers ago and I was helping them unpack, I discovered she had moved a pint of expired buttermilk from the old house to the new one. I found it on ice. In a cooler. Because until that buttermilk is curdled, it's pretty much fair game.

But I digress.

After some brainstorming, Mama and I decided that there was a simple solution to the problem—one that would significantly increase Daddy's fashion IQ *and* save the sweater. Mama would simply cover the hole by performing an emblem transplant. She would carefully remove an alligator from one of my brother's tattered Izod shirts and then introduce the alligator to a new habitat: Daddy's sweater. It required some careful cutting and stitching on Mama's part, but in the end she was able to salvage the blue sweater. I was tickled by Mama's ingenuity, and while Daddy was none the wiser, he was destined to be so much more stylish. Or so we thought.

Two weeks later Daddy was on TV again, this time to explain the proper way to root a cutting from a hydrangea or fertilize an azalea or whatever. Naturally he was wearing The Sweater, and Mama and I were understandably relieved since it was now sporting an alligator instead of the much-maligned fox. The emblem switcheroo had been so simple—sly as a fox, you might say—until the camera zoomed in for a close-up of whatever Daddy was holding.

Then we saw it. And we froze.

Because the alligator, you see, was upside down, plain as day and larger than life on the six o'clock news. It was simultaneously hilarious and mortifying, especially since it halfway looked like some sort of Cooperative Extension Service gang sign, warning all the 4-H agents who favor polo players on their shirts that the county agents who wear alligators DON'T MESS AROUND.

All I could do was gesture in the general direction of the TV screen and say, "Mama. Mama? MAMA!"

When she realized that the alligator was about 180 degrees off its target, she just shook her head and said, "Well, that figures."

And she was right. It *did* figure. Because designer brands and Daddy just don't go together. The upside-down alligator taught us that lesson once and for all. And I have to admit that life has been better and easier since we all accepted that Daddy's idea of high fashion is a sweater with an ailing fox or, perhaps, the wrinkle-resistant khakis from the George collection at Walmart. Daddy doesn't need the latest from Tommy Bahama for his golf outings, because he would just as soon wear a line from Sears called Jimmy Barbados.

Not that Jimmy Barbados is an actual fashion line. But if it were, Daddy would be all over it, especially if the most expensive item in the collection was somewhere in the vicinity of $19.99.

🌷

So yes, Mama and Daddy had weathered the occasional sartorial storm, but it didn't seem like Daddy's clothes were the real problem in the article about him and Mrs. Cunningham. There was something deeper. And after I'd listened to Mama vent her exasperation to Chox for several more minutes, I finally got a clearer picture of what was *really* going on.

"Well," Mama continued, "I cannot believe that my husband would go outside of this house . . ."

As she searched for the right words, she twisted the phone cord and sat down at the desk chair in the kitchen.

"I cannot believe that my husband—*my husband*—would go outside of this house *to learn how to make biscuits*. The very idea! The very idea that *I* couldn't teach him to make biscuits! I've been making homemade biscuits since I was knee high to a grasshopper, but has he ever wanted to learn from me? Nooooooo. And now it's in the paper? And there are pictures? And people will think that he couldn't have just stayed home and learned how to make biscuits from me? Quite frankly, *I don't appreciate it one bit.*"

And there was the rub. It wasn't that Daddy didn't pay attention to what clothes he was wearing. It wasn't that Daddy didn't tell her about the article beforehand. It was that after thirty years of marriage, after thirty years of dishing out three hot meals a day, Mama very rightly considered herself a fine Southern cook, and by golly if Daddy wanted to learn to make biscuits, he should have come to her for the privilege.

Mama stood in total agreement with the county-wide assessment that Mrs. Cunningham was a wonderful cook—there were no arguments from her on that count—but what troubled her was that some people might assume Daddy had to learn how to make biscuits from Mrs. Cunningham because *Mama didn't know how.*

By all means, let me err on the side of being exceedingly clear:

my mama is not a petty woman. She's not a drama queen. I've watched her politely hold her tongue in situations where the good Lord Himself would have been tempted to read someone the riot act. But over the years I've realized that marriages are the sum of thousands of symbolic parts, and Mama's disappointment about the biscuits was no doubt about way more than, well, *biscuits*. So when you combine whatever subtext was going on with the mathematical reality of how many times Mama had proved her biscuit-making skills over the course of their marriage, the end result of that equation was a wife with some hurt feelings.

And now that I'm older? With fifteen-plus years of marriage under my own belt? I absolutely get it. Sometimes a perceived slight stings more than an intentional one ever could. If you don't believe me, then remind me to tell you about the time when David and I were on the way home from the hospital with our newborn little boy, and I thought David asked me what I was going to cook for supper.

I'd never been angrier.

I'd also heard him wrong, but the deficiency in my listening skills did not negate the fact that I THOUGHT HE ASKED ME WHAT I WAS GOING TO COOK FOR SUPPER.

AND I WAS RECOVERING FROM A C-SECTION.

AND THERE WAS A THREE-DAY-OLD IN THE BACKSEAT.

But I'm totally over it.

I recently asked Mama if she ever brought up The Biscuit Ordeal to Daddy, and she assured me that she hadn't. "Sometimes," she said, "you just have to ask the Lord to help you make your peace with things and move on. Your daddy didn't mean anything by it, and it didn't make good sense for me to hold a grudge."

She's right, of course. Occasionally in marriage you have to pick your battles, and ultimately Mama decided the biscuits weren't worth an argument. As C. S. Lewis once wrote, "Love . . . is not merely a feeling. It is a deep unity, maintained by the will and deliberately strengthened by habit; reinforced by (in Christian marriage) the grace which both partners ask, and receive, from God."

Mama could've given Daddy a hard time, but instead she gave him grace. I looked over at Mama, and just as I was about to ponder the blessing and the legacy of Proverbs 31:10, of "an excellent wife . . . [who is] far more precious than jewels," I remembered one more pesky detail I wanted to ask her about.

"Mama?" I asked. "Remember the Christmas after Daddy learned to make the biscuits? And remember how he got up early on Christmas morning and made biscuits for everybody?"

"I do remember that," she replied.

"Well," I continued, "I may have the story mixed up, but I don't think you ate any of those biscuits. You smiled, and you talked about how delicious they looked, but you didn't touch so much as a crumb. You made sure everybody had jelly and syrup, but you didn't take a single bite. Why was that?"

Mama grinned. "Honey, I knew your daddy didn't mean any harm. Mrs. Cunningham did a wonderful job teaching him, but you and I both know he could've learned to make those biscuits from me if he'd only thought to ask. I just wanted to stand on my principles a little bit."

"And besides," she added, "your daddy was so proud that he'd made biscuits for y'all on Christmas morning. It never occurred to him that I didn't try them. And we had such a merry Christmas that year—whether I ate those biscuits or not."

She was right, of course. We did have a merry Christmas.

And even though Mama didn't eat the biscuits, she didn't have to cook breakfast, either. Which meant she only prepared breakfast 349 times that year as opposed to her normal 350.

I think she'd consider that a win.

CHAPTER FIVE

When the "Immeasurably More" Pretty Much Rocks Your World

WHEN I WAS GROWING UP, I was a fairly typical little Southern girl. I wore pretty dresses that were trimmed in lace or rickrack (sometimes both); I played outside for hours with my neighbors; I always let Mama wash and roll my hair on Saturday nights so it would be extra clean and curly for church on Sunday mornings. I took piano lessons; I performed in dance recitals; I learned to say, "Yes, ma'am" and "Yes, sir" and "No, ma'am" and "No, sir" to my elders. And even when they didn't know it, I paid attention to every move the women in my family made when they were getting ready for big Sunday dinners.

Oh, listen. I'm pretty sure I earned a degree in Southern Table Setting just from watching Mamaw Davis, Mama, Chox, Sister, and an assortment of cousins carefully place china, crystal, and sterling silver on the dining room table of whoever happened to be hosting dinner that week. When Paige and I were finally old enough to be trusted with setting the table ourselves, we had the routine down pat. We knew where Mama and Chox kept their silver chests, we knew how to put the leaf in Mama's dining room table, we knew where to find the pressed linens, and we knew to be extra careful with the good china.

Watching and learning from Mama and the other women in my family gave me a deep love for home and hearth and taking care of people. I knew from a young age that there was eternal value in those things, and I treasured the moments when Mama let me help her look after our guests. I vividly remember the first time Mama asked me to make a pot of coffee for her and her friends, just as I remember the first time Chox asked me to serve at a bridal tea for a family friend. Like Scout Finch in *To Kill a Mockingbird*, I saw the effortless grace and elegance of the women around me and realized that "there was some skill involved in being a girl," and I knew I didn't just want to grow up and be a woman.

I wanted to grow up and be a lady.

Given all of that, it strikes me as sort of interesting that despite the fact that I was a girly girl who loved bows and frills and makeup and clothes, and despite the fact that I couldn't wait to grow up and get married and take care of my husband and have a house of my own, I never really dreamed of being a mother.

Certainly I admired and esteemed mothers. There's no question about that. And I loved my own mama beyond all comprehension.

I just didn't, you know, want to *be* one. Maybe it was because I was the baby of my family by ten years and never experienced taking care of younger siblings. Maybe it was because I tended to gravitate to adults instead of kids when I was a child. Maybe it was because, on some level, I felt like Mama had sacrificed a lot of her own dreams to make sure that my sister, my brother, and I had the opportunity to pursue ours. Or maybe it was some combination of all three.

Regardless, I just didn't have the expectant enthusiasm about eventually being a mama that many girls feel when they're young. I did enjoy dolls in the sense that they were nice to look at and all that, but mostly I just liked to have my dolls nap in my room while I sat with Mama on the couch in the den and watched *Guiding Light* and *Match Game*.

Call me crazy, but that tendency didn't necessarily scream SOLID MATERNAL INSTINCTS.

Even when my childhood best friend, Laura, and I would talk about what we wanted to be when we grew up, mothering rarely entered the conversation for me. I loved to dream about being someone who operated a cash register in a cute store or someone who answered a push-button phone and then transferred calls with great efficiency or someone who typed with urgency on an IBM Selectric and then filed lots of important documents.

Later, when I was a teenager, I just wanted to be Jane Craig from *Broadcast News* and scream, "Lay it in, Bobby! Back it up!" before handing a news segment tape to Joan Cusack as she barreled down the hall on her way to the control room.

So basically I think what we've established is that all my dreams involved mashing buttons.

SHOOT FOR THE STARS, YOUNG PEOPLE.

My only concession to Thoughts of Motherhood was a fairly significant obsession with children's names. Even now I'm fascinated by why people choose certain names for their kids—why they name a daughter Kaitlyn or Katelin or Catelyn, why they name a son Robert Hughes Von Pritchett IV and then elect to call him "Bo." And when I was younger, every once in a while

I'd think about hypothetical children and wonder if it would be better to name a little girl Mary Margaret or Lucy Katherine or Emma Paige or Anna Clair (a double name was a given; the fact that I didn't have one myself was, in my opinion, one of life's great injustices).

What I never thought about, though, was what it would be like to *mother* those children. I guess the bottom line was that I didn't really have a desire to be a mama, but if a friend or two would grant me naming privileges when they had kids of their own, then that would probably work out really well for everybody. Especially since I would try my best to come up with a universal spelling of Caitlin and thereby provide a valuable public service to frustrated schoolteachers everywhere.

I'm leaning toward Keightlynne, but I'll keep you posted.

During my college years I definitely warmed up to children in general, but when I'd hear my friends talk about how they'd love to have two or three or six kids one day, I didn't get it. AT ALL. Didn't they want to be Jane Craig? Didn't they want to travel? Didn't they want to be able to stay up half the night watching old John Hughes movies without having someone who, like, *depended* on them?

My reasoning was totally flawed, of course. I saw a life with kids and a life that was fun and fulfilling as two separate entities. In my mind it was an either-or decision. I had no idea it could be an also-and choice. We can unpack this idea more extensively when we meet at my counselor's office next week. You can just add it to our discussion list, right after "ongoing issues with repetitive circular textures" and "profound fear of clowns."

But.

(You knew it was coming, didn't you?)

(OF COURSE YOU DID.)

When I was twenty-three or twenty-four, I think, smack-dab in the middle of the ickiest phase of my whole life, one of my very best friends, Elise, gave birth to her first baby. I'll never forget talking to Elise on the phone, standing in the middle of my parents' kitchen, and marveling at the pure, unadulterated joy in her voice. After I told her how thrilled I was for her and her husband and how I knew they were going to be the best parents any little boy could want, I hung up the phone, stood in silence for a few seconds, and then I cried my eyes out.

It was the full-on, ugly, ma'am-can-somebody-get-you-a-sedative cry. And while I wasn't exactly sure what part of my conversation with Elise moved me to tears, I suspected it had something to do with the fact that she had completely surrendered herself to somebody besides herself. I'd heard about doing that in response to God for most of my life, but I don't think I'd ever realized the deep, sacrificial nature of a parent's love until I heard it in Elise's voice. And somehow, in some deep-down place inside me, it changed me.

God changed me.

I didn't realize it in that moment, of course. That phone call was really just the tiniest step onto a long bridge. I had to walk that bridge for a year (or eight) before I could turn around and see that my viewpoint had changed.

※

When David and I started dating seriously, we talked about kids. I think that's pretty standard conversational fare when you're realizing that you're going to spend the rest of your life with somebody. We were twenty-six-ish, I think, and neither of us had nieces or nephews—an interesting detail for two people who are the babies in their families by a country mile. I don't remember

41

our being completely opposed to the idea of kids, but I don't remember being gung ho, either. We both wanted to enjoy married life and go on great vacations and live in cool houses. I even told a friend of mine that I probably wouldn't have children because I was a teacher and the last thing I'd want to do was leave high school kids in the afternoon and then have to go home and take care of my own.

Good point, Captain Wisdom. Because those relationships are totally the same thing.

And to be clear: I don't think parenthood is a given for everybody. Neither is marriage. God's going to use all of us differently. It just tickles me that I thought I had it all figured out when I was neither a wife nor a parent. And when I was barely old enough to rent a car, for that matter.

After David and I got married, we honestly didn't talk much about kids for quite some time. Both of us had lived on our own for six years after college, so after we married, we spent a lot of time trying to adjust to (1) sleeping in a bed with another person, (2) living with another person, (3) checking with another person before making dinner plans with friends, (4) learning not to snap at another person because the togetherness can be exhausting, and (5) wondering how anyone ever makes it through the first year of marriage because that is a LOT of time with another person.

We really did love each other.

But we really did drive each other crazy.

Maybe one day, if I have the strength, I will tell you about the night David threw his bag of tortilla chips at the kitchen wall because I wanted him to share them with me.

It was almost exactly like one of those tender Hallmark card moments, except that it wasn't.

Here's the thing: having a wedding is easy, but being married is hard. Considering that David and I had ambled into marriage thinking *maybe* we had a little bit of emotional baggage that we were going to have to deal with—only to find out that we'd each brought several extra-large, customized steamer trunks filled with barbells as well as a kicky assortment of lead—we didn't have an easy go of it for the first three years. And when we finally started to unpack those steamer trunks after our third anniversary, we had no idea that the unpacking and the dealing and the healing would take another couple of years.

So by year five, when we were in our early thirties and most of our friends had two or maybe even three kids (and my friend Wendi had four. FOUR!), we were just thankful to have a marriage that was still intact. We'd moved to Birmingham, a place that immediately felt like home to both of us, and we had started to use the *b* word ("baby") a *little* bit more. However, I still couldn't wrap my head around the reality of having a child living in our house. I couldn't wrap my head around the reality of having a child growing in my body. After all, there are only a couple of options in terms of getting a baby out, and I couldn't really get on board with either of them.

In the summer of 2002 I went to the doctor for my yearly checkup. When I mentioned that David and I were talking a little more about having a baby, the doctor looked over my chart, told me to be sure to take my vitamins, and before I left his office, gave me the go-ahead to "start trying," an expression that makes my skin crawl a little bit. Maybe I'm too uptight about it, but whenever someone says they're going to "start trying," I'm always mindful that what they're actually saying is, "Oh, we are about to start having A LOT OF SEX in our house." Quite frankly that is just way more information than I need.

A few weeks later, David and I went to Myrtlewood for several days so we could celebrate Martha's birthday. We'd asked her to make a list of jobs she wanted done around the house—she and Sissie lived together, but neither one of them had any business being on a ladder, you understand—and we planned to spend a long weekend painting and planting and trying to check a few things off Martha's list. I thought on the drive over that I felt a little queasy—not sick, exactly, though definitely not normal—but I chalked it up to carsickness and ate a few crackers.

I think for normal people the uncharacteristic nausea probably would have been a clue that MA'AM, YOU COULD VERY WELL BE WITH CHILD, but the thought barely crossed my mind. After all, it had only been about three weeks since I'd seen the doctor, and I'd already decided that if we ever got really serious about having a baby, it would no doubt take me a sweet forever to get pregnant.

Yes. I *decided*.

Welcome to my crazy. I hope you enjoy your stay.

The nausea ebbed and flowed while we were at Martha's, and by the time we got back to Birmingham, I had a pretty strong suspicion that I was gonna be a mama to somebody besides our dogs. I didn't want to take a pregnancy test, though, because I kind of enjoyed dwelling in the Land of Not Knowing. I realize that probably sounds absolutely ludicrous, but on some level I was scared to get my hopes up. I had mastered the fine art of waiting for the other shoe to drop, so a baby? That soon? When I'd spent the better part of twenty-five years thinking I wasn't the motherly type?

I seriously could not fathom that the Lord would be that gracious to me. Could not fathom it.

But He was. The doctor confirmed it (after I took a home pregnancy test and *decided* that there was no way that it could be accurate). I was due in March. Finding out was one of the sweetest moments of my whole life, mainly because it was one of the most unexpected moments of my whole life.

God is so much better than I deserve.

My pregnancy was a fairly standard affair, and I did my best to soak up every second. Since I'd never thought much about what it would feel like to actually be pregnant, the whole experience was just astonishing to me. Whether it was hearing the heartbeat, finding out we were having a boy, feeling him kick, or picking out fabric for the nursery, I basically spent the better part of eight months wanting to say, "PEOPLE! THIS PREGNANCY THING? WHY DIDN'T ANYBODY TELL ME? THIS IS DELIGHTFUL!"

You may have picked up on the fact that I tend to operate at extremes. I'm either fighting my way through vehement opposition or trying to convince everybody I know that I have single-handedly discovered the most awesome awesomeness the world has to offer.

It's a very charming and endearing quality, as I'm sure you can imagine. And it's not at all annoying. Not at all.

As much as I loved those first eight months of pregnancy, I have to admit that I was a *sight* by February. I felt like my belly started just below my throat and ended right above my knees. My lips looked like I'd had a run-in with an economy-sized vial of Restylane, and when I talked I sounded like a swollen duck, only significantly less melodious than one would imagine a swollen duck to be. My feet were basically planks, and on a good day I could wedge them into some bedroom slippers or maybe even some extra-wide flats I'd picked up at the Payless. I wasn't at all sure I'd ever see my ankles again. Plus, going to sleep was a joke since there was absolutely no way to get comfortable, and on the off chance that I dozed off for longer than an hour, my unique oh-sweet-mercy-is-there-a-wounded-animal-in-the-house brand of snoring would inevitably jar me from my fitful slumber.

But before I knew it, it was a Friday morning in mid-March, and as the first hint of sunlight came over the horizon, David and I climbed in the car (Okay. I'll be honest. I *hoisted* myself in the car) and drove to the hospital. I was terrified. David was practically doing somersaults in the front seat, and I think if I hadn't been so busy crying, I probably would've punched him (gently) in the arm. After all, I was a smidge overwhelmed by what being a mama would entail, and I needed to have my final pre-baby breakdown without his unbridled enthusiasm working overtime to cheer me up.

Bless his heart.

Trying to anticipate and diffuse my ever-changing moods was a losing battle, but that didn't stop him from fighting the good fight.

When we finally arrived at the hospital, my nerves all but vanished. I became immeasurably calmer, which no doubt had everything to do with medication. I had a scheduled C-section, and before I knew it, our sweet nurse was praying over us and then wheeling me back to the surgery suite. You probably shouldn't quote me on this, but I'm pretty sure that they call it a "suite" so patients will get distracted by the luxurious terminology and forget about all the Sharp Medical Instruments and Bloodsucking Machines that await them on the other side of those swinging doors.

That is merely my own personal theory. By all means feel free to dismiss it if you prefer to think of the suite as an extra-large room at the Westin, complete with a heavenly bed, a high-definition television, and round-the-clock complimentary room service.

About thirty minutes after my epidural, and after some significant tugging and pulling (I also assume there was some cutting, but I choose not to think about that part), my wonderful doctor held up a beautiful, bawling baby boy who was essentially a three-month-old. Ten pounds, seven ounces. Nearly twenty-three inches. Gorgeous. Perfect. Surreal.

I wondered if I'd catch my first glimpse of Alex and we'd have an "amazing connection" like all those mamas on TLC's *A Baby Story* who give birth without the aid of anesthesia in large round tubs filled with water while the whole family looks on. Those shows always astound me, because while the expectant mama contorts herself over the back of a sofa, dilated to six centimeters and trying not to pass out from the pain, the kids are all standing at the front door, handing a Domino's delivery guy some cash and then getting back to the important business of their intrafamily Wii Sports Resort tournament. The mama looks at her older children with great love and affection, then shakes her head as if to say, "Oh, those crazy kids," despite the fact that her contractions have amped up to Mach 10 and her husband is still in the kitchen digging through the medicine cabinet for some ibuprofen.

Because when it comes to dulling the agony of full-blown labor, ibuprofen is just the medicinal ticket.

I mean, I know full well that I'm a medical coward and all, but after Alex was born and my back was killing me and the doctors were tending to the somewhat essential business of putting me back together again, ibuprofen was the last thing on my mind.

But a morphine pump?

Oh, now you're talking. Yes, please, and thank you. I believe I will.

And as it turned out, Alex and I didn't really have time for an "amazing connection" since I still needed an assortment of staples and stitches. So once I saw him, kissed his little forehead, pronounced that he looked exactly like my older nephew, and knew that he was healthy, I was perfectly fine letting David take over for a few minutes while I got some relief (Heyyyyyyy, morphine pump!) and the doctors returned all my organs to their proper places. I'm practical like that.

About fifteen minutes later, when the little man was all cleaned up and I was back in the recovery room, the nurse finally placed him in my arms. I was mesmerized. It had nothing to do with the fact that I had been carrying him for nine months, but it had everything to do with the realization that he was a wonder, a gift, and—as trite as it may sound—a miracle. I loved him instantly, and I was deeply, profoundly humbled by the realization that as much as I loved Alex in that moment, it was just an infinitesimal fraction of how much God loves us. It was an instantaneous, profound, life-altering shift in perspective.

That baby boy changed everything for me. And in all the best ways.

The next couple of days flew by in a blur of family and friends and baby love. I developed a special bond with the crushed ice on the maternity floor and was apparently so obsessed with it that I announced to anyone who would listen that the ice was extra delicious because while it had the same consistency as the crushed ice at Sonic, size-wise it was more like the crushed ice at Hardee's (Heyyyyyyy, morphine pump!).

That weekend also happened to be the Southeastern Conference men's basketball tournament. My beloved Mississippi

State Bulldogs had made it to the championship game, so when I wasn't holding or nursing or cooing at my baby, I spent a great deal of time screaming, "BLOCK OUT!" and "REBOUND!" and "PASS THE BALL!" while simultaneously setting off the alarm on my blood pressure monitor.

Welcome to the world, Alex Hudson. It's better if you know from the get-go that your mama believes way down in her soul that the Bulldogs can hear her yelling through the TV.

Sunday night was our last night in the hospital, and since I was starting to feel more like myself again (So long, morphine pump!), I asked David if he'd pick up some nonhospital food for supper and then head home for the night to make sure that our dogs were okay.

He returned to the hospital with Mexican food, which was such a thoughtful gesture since I love Mexican food almost as much as I love fried chicken. Unfortunately, David didn't realize I had to avoid spicy food since I was nursing the baby, so I pushed all the good stuff to the side and enjoyed a delicious corn tortilla for supper. It was just like *The Rime of the Ancient Mariner*: tacos, tacos, everywhere / but ne'er a bean to eat.

We had a real good laugh about it once my postpartum hormones decided it was funny.

After David went home, Alex decided he was hungry, so I fed him and thought it would be nice for the two of us to visit for a little while. It was the first time we'd been by ourselves when he was awake, and as I sat in that squishy vinyl hospital chair and stared at what was surely the most precious face I had ever seen, I told that little man how much I loved him, how often I'd prayed for him, how thankful I was for the privilege of being his mama. And I thought about my very favorite passage of Scripture—one I'd committed to memory when I was seventeen years old and had no idea how faithful the Lord would be through the struggles and wonders and heartaches and joys that lay ahead: "Now to him who is able to do immeasurably more than all we ask or imagine, according to his power that is at work within us, to him be glory in the church and in Christ Jesus throughout all generations, for ever and ever" (Ephesians 3:20-21, NIV).

And then I cried. Because having a child—being a family— was an "immeasurably more" moment for me. I was overcome with gratitude that God had given us the gift of this sweet baby— a gift that, for most of my life, I had no idea I wanted.

Alex cried, too, by the way. But I think it was because he had a dirty diaper.

I snapped out of my tearful reverie and gingerly stood up from the chair. I grabbed a diaper, changed the little man, and after a little swaying, a little singing, and a little swaddling, I put him in his bassinette. And y'all, he went straight to sleep.

He totally did.

Well, what do you know? I thought. *Maybe I do have some maternal instincts after all.*

That's the thing about the "immeasurably more." God prepares you for it even when it's nowhere on your to-do list.

And now that I have the benefit of looking at my childhood through a lens with some wisdom attached, it occurs to me that during all those Sunday dinners when I was growing up, I learned something way more important than how to make a pitcher of sweet tea or where to put the salad fork or when to pick up dinner plates before Mama served dessert. I learned something more important than how to be a lady, even.

I learned to listen and to laugh. I learned to forgive. I learned that some earthly love really is unconditional. I learned that God is always at work in the day to day. I learned that even when you're sad or embarrassed or just plain mad, you're always welcome at the table.

And more than anything else, I learned how to take care of people. I learned how to let them take care of me. I learned how to be a family.

I didn't have the slightest clue that anyone was teaching me, of course.

But I'm forever grateful for the lesson.

CHAPTER SIX

Mother's Got a Bell! A Ringy-Ding Bell!

W<small>HEN</small> S<small>ISSIE</small> <small>WAS</small> <small>ABOUT</small> ninety-five years young, she fell and broke her hip. The ensuing hospital stay was a lengthy one, and once Sissie finally returned home, Martha realized that she was going to need some extra help to take care of her mother. She decided on a local home health service, and while the bulk of the Sissie-related responsibilities still fell on Martha's shoulders, she was able to schedule sitters for a few hours every day so she could run to the grocery store, go to church, or meet friends for lunch. Martha's attentiveness to Sissie's care demonstrated a level of devotion that would make Florence Nightingale say, "Dang—I need to step up my game," so whenever Martha would leave the house, she always made sure that there was a small, handheld bell beside Sissie's bed. Just in case Sissie needed to ring it for some immediate attention, you understand.

One of Martha's favorite annual events has always been her Sunday school class's Christmas party, and even though she was absolutely exhausted and could barely wrap her brain around putting on a sparkly three-quarter-sleeve jacket with some dressy slacks and spending the evening at the country club, she figured it would be good for her spirits to spend a few hours with her friends. Martha went to great pains to schedule a sitter—not an easy feat during the holidays—and before she left the house, she made sure to tell Sissie that someone else was there to help.

"Mother, you ring your bell if you need anything! If you need *anything*! The sitter will be sure to help you with whatever you need, and I'll be home in a few hours. Okay, sugar? You get some good rest, sugar."

Martha felt fine about the arrangement as she backed out of the carport, but when she got home "a little before nine, I was home before nine! I wasn't even out that late!" she was distressed to find the sitter sound asleep—snoring, even—in the living room recliner. Despite her first inclination to let sleeping sitters lie, Martha's concern for Sissie proved too strong to ignore. She wanted to check with the sitter to make sure everything was okay with Sissie, and that's why Martha stood in front of the recliner for the better part of five minutes and repeated, at varying volumes, some variation of "Hello! Hey there! Time to wake up! I'm home now! It's time to get up! I want to ask you about my mother! Hey, honey! Hello!"

The sitter never budged. She didn't miss a beat with her snoring, either.

I'd like to think that if I had been in Martha's position at this juncture, I would have walked over to the woman in the recliner, put my hand on her shoulder, and very gently said something like "WAKE UP! WAKE UP! YOU'RE ON THE CLOCK, AND I'M NOT PAYING YOU TO SLEEP, MA'AM." But

Martha avoids confrontation of any sort, so here is what she did in an attempt to rouse the sleeping sitter:

1. Walked in the master bedroom and shut the door.
2. Opened the door.
3. Walked in the master bathroom and shut the door.
4. Opened the door.
5. Flushed the commode.
6. Walked in the kitchen, where she repeatedly opened and shut the door to the microwave because, according to Martha, "My microwave door is really loud! It's terribly loud! And I don't see how anybody could sleep through me shutting it, especially not over and over again!"

At that point Sissie woke up (no doubt because of that microwave door opening and shutting), so she started ringing her bell and yelling, "MAH-THA! MAHHHHHH-THA!" as loudly as she could. The sitter still didn't move, and according to Martha, "She didn't even hear Mother's bell! She didn't hear the bell! And you know I was at the Sunday school party, and what if Mother needed her and rang the bell and the sitter never answered? What if she never answered? Because she surely didn't hear it when I was home! She didn't! Mother rang her bell, and the sitter never heard it!"

And then, after a brief pause: "CAN YOU EVEN IMAGINE?"

So Martha took care of whatever Sissie needed before she walked in the living room and stood in front of the recliner and loudly cleared her throat four or eleventy hundred times until the sitter finally stirred. And instead of asking the sitter what in the world she was thinking, Martha simply said, "I couldn't get you to wake up! Mother even rang her bell! And I opened and closed the microwave door!"

I'm going to venture a guess that the sitter no doubt wondered how she'd fallen asleep in Myrtlewood only to wake up smack-dab in the middle of a Tennessee Williams play.

The sleeping sitter confessed that she had been a bit sick to her stomach earlier in the evening and had taken an anti-nausea pill or two, and much to her surprise she became incredibly drowsy and dozed off into what might be classified as a light coma. Martha told her that it probably wasn't a good idea to take medication when she had a job that required *staying awake in order to care for the elderly*, but the sitter was nonplussed and asked Martha if she could have her check, seeing as how she had some Christmas shopping to do the next day.

I'd be willing to bet that Martha probably cleared her throat about fifty-four more times after that request. She was going to be polite at all costs, of course, but she had to consider her mama's best interests. And before the sitter left, Martha managed to tell her that it just wasn't going to work out. She was a perfectly lovely person and all—perfectly lovely!—but Martha needed to know that Sissie was in good hands.

I mean, sleeping on the job was one thing.

Being oblivious to the sound of the microwave door was another.

But failing to hear Sissie's bell? That was a deal breaker, my friends.

CHAPTER SEVEN

The Night We neither Camped nor Fished

WAY BACK IN THE DARK ages of 2005, my husband and I went to Myrtlewood to celebrate Christmas with our families. We took Alex with us, too, since he was two and a half and couldn't really stay home by himself yet. Plus, we were pretty exhausted from all the holiday goings-on and needed Alex to drive that first leg of the trip from Birmingham to Tuscaloosa.

Listen. Don't laugh. He still needed a little work on his defensive driving skills, but he could flat let 'er rip once he hit the interstate. Sure, he got a little tired somewhere around the Bessemer exit and really wanted to snuggle with Froggy, but it was nothing a stiff cup of Starbucks couldn't fix.

Anyway, since the Hudson Christmas Extravaganza was on a Saturday, David and I made plans to go to dinner that Friday night with my mama and daddy. My aunt and uncle were going, too, but our little guy stayed with Martha. We really wanted to take him with us, but we didn't think he was quite ready to drive in the dark.

(Apparently I'm going to keep going back to that whole toddler driving setup.)

(It makes me laugh.)

(Probably because I have such a mature sense of humor.)

When we were trying to decide where to go to eat, we eventually arrived at the conclusion that we were all craving fried catfish, and that means, at least in parts of Mississippi, that you hop in the car and head to "the fish camp."

I'm not exactly sure how the whole fish camp phenomenon started, but I think it had something to do with people setting up camp along central Mississippi rivers and then frying up their catch once the sun set. Since I personally prefer to partake of my meals in a room that's sealed off from all the nature, I'm thankful that the tradition hasn't stayed outside on the riverbank. These days people build cabins and furnish them with an endless stretch of picnic tables, and then a steady crowd of happy, um, *campers* show up on weekend nights to enjoy fried fish, french fries, hush puppies, coleslaw, and sweet tea. Some fish camps even serve boiled shrimp or crab legs or fresh oysters, but that's only if they're high end. And really, if you think about it, a high-end fish camp sort of defeats the whole point.

Before we went to supper on that particular night, we met at Chox and Joe's house, and just so we can address what you've probably been thinking since the first chapter, I'll go ahead and affirm that yes, you certainly have been reading correctly: *my uncle's name is Joe.* I know, it's very unusual.

Seriously, though, my aunt's name really is Choxie. Chox, for short. She and my mama actually had an aunt—their daddy's sister—by the same name. When Chox was born, her deep, olive-colored skin tone favored the elder Choxie, so Mamaw and Papaw decided she should also inherit the name. About thirty years later Chox gave birth to my cousin Choxie Paige (who goes by Paige but is a Choxie through and through).

Since I grew up surrounded by Choxies, I haven't spent a lot of time thinking about what an unusual name it is. Then again, I come from a long line of people with names like Maude, Roxie, Tom Alex, Levert, Alma, and Ouida. So having a Chox or three in the family? Well, that's perfectly normal. Perhaps there will be a time when I can also tell you about my daddy's aunt Cecil.

Good grief, I love the South.

Anyway, we met at Chox and Joe's house, mainly because we all wanted to ride in the same car and Chox's SUV was the biggest of the bunch. Plus, at the time, Joe was in the early stages of Alzheimer's, and generally there was a better chance he'd know where we were and who we were if we left from their house. It was just less confusing all the way around. And trust me: I'm not trying to be blasé about Joe's Alzheimer's; that's just how my family rolls when it comes to Big Life Developments. My sister and I laugh about how, when we were growing up, our polar-opposite-of-helicopter parents looked at every hardship as an opportunity to work harder and trust God more deeply. Sister and I refer to this as the "get after it" approach to life, and I am here to tell you that my brother, my sister, and I inherited this mind-set IN SPADES.

Unexpected changes at work? Well, take a day to be sad—and then get after it.

Challenges in your marriage? Talk about the problems—and then get after it.

Hardships with your health? Get the help you need—and then, as best as you can, get after it.

The "get after it" approach doesn't mean you have to be cold or insensitive or hard hearted, but it very much means that the good Lord never puts more on your plate than you can handle, so you just, with His guidance, try to find the best plan of attack for every single problem, and then, well, you get after it.

That's precisely why, when Joe was diagnosed with Alzheimer's, we all knew that we wouldn't hear a word of self-pity or "Why us?" from Chox about what they were facing. She simply asked the Lord for strength to get through every single day, gathered as much information as she could, tried to keep Joe as happy and comfortable as possible, and then, well, she got after it. They'd built a business together, as well as a mighty fine marriage, and she became the primary champion of both. There were times when I thought I'd never seen anyone look as tired as she did, but she never complained. No, sir. She just got after it.

(Remind me to tell you about the time my sister's house flooded.)

(That, I have to say, was some of the finest gettin'-after-it my family has ever seen.)

Our trip to the fish camp coincided with a patch of time when Joe was beginning to get really confused about who was who and what was what; his and Chox's house was littered with slips of paper where he wrote down bits and pieces of information that he was trying to convince his brain to remember. He would jot down the dates of his service in the Marines, the name of a neighborhood friend from his childhood, the price of a printing press from 1974—whatever came to mind. Paige often found those little scraps of her daddy's memory written inside a telephone book, on the back of a deposit slip, or on the corner of a manila envelope, and inevitably she'd smile as she wiped away her tears.

When David and I walked in the front door at Chox and Joe's that Friday night, I could tell by the look on Joe's face that he knew he was *supposed* to know who we were; he seemed to have a sense that we were, at the very least, familiar to him, though he couldn't seem to put all the relational pieces together. Chox made a point to nonchalantly announce our arrival in front of him—"Oh, look who's here from Alabama! It's Soph and David!" In doing so, she saved him the embarrassment and frustration of not being able to remember our names right away. The great thing about Joe, bless his heart, was that he was always just as enthusiastic as could be when he saw pretty much anybody. That was true before Alzheimer's set in, and it was true afterward, too. He might not have had the foggiest idea who he was talking to, but by diggity, his enthusiasm for talking to that person was unshakable. That night was no exception.

Once Mama and Daddy arrived, we all piled into Chox's SUV to make the pilgrimage to our fried-fish paradise. For some reason I was appointed chauffeur for the evening, so I climbed in the driver's seat, waited for everybody to buckle up, and backed out of the driveway. I reminded myself not to drive too fast on the way to the fish camp, but those hush puppies were calling my name, and the time, it was a-wastin'. I mean, normally I do my best to be a conscientious driver and put safety first and all that, but there's something about the prospect of a night filled with fried food that makes me want to throw all reason out the window and *giddyup*.

The first part of our trip was relatively uneventful. Mama and Chox took care of most of the talking during our thirty-minute car ride, focusing primarily on a little conversational segment I like to refer to as People We Know Who Have Died. The best part of any People We Know Who Have Died (PWKWHD for short) conversation is the inevitable constructive criticism/ evaluation of the funeral service, centering on (1) the quality of the music, (2) the finish of the casket, and (3) the appropri- ateness of the attendees' attire. In Myrtlewood you can almost always count on the music being beautiful and the casket finish being tasteful, but people's funeral fashion choices are increasingly problematic for Mama and Chox. Opt for a conservative pantsuit or a Sunday dress, and they will sing your praises. Show up in your tennis clothes, and prepare to be a topic of some PWKWHD conversations. All in the interest of exhortation and edification, of course.

And if you show up in jeans, I guess the good news is that they actually won't talk about you at all. Because as far as they're concerned, your ancestors are to blame for that one. It certainly isn't *your* fault if you're mired in a generational stronghold that makes you overly dependent on denim.

Once they'd made their way through PWKWHD, Mama and Chox segued into People We Know Who Are Sick and/or Injured, followed closely by my favorite portion of the conversational proceedings: Well, That's What I Heard.

"Ouida, did you know that Sue Jones moved to Knoxville?"

"Tennessee? No! I had no idea!"

"Well, that's what I heard."

Or this:

"Chox, has anybody mentioned to you that they're getting a new preacher at that Baptist church over by the park?"

"Really? Isn't their preacher from down in south Alabama? The one with that darlin' wife who's expecting again? Seems like he's only been there for about two years. He's leaving already?"

"Well, that's what I heard."

I could clap my hands just thinking about it.

We arrived at the fish camp not too long after the matter

regarding the Baptist preacher was settled, and once I found
a parking place underneath an old oak tree, everybody gradually filed out of the car. Daddy's knees were a little resentful of
the time he'd been sitting still, as was Chox's hip, so once all
the necessary limbs were sufficiently stretched and restored to
good working order, we dodged some impressive tree roots and
crunched our way through the gravel parking lot.

Now, in the event you should ever find yourself at a Mississippi
fish camp on a random weekend night, I'm going to share a little
piece of information that I hope will prepare you for the experience: I have noticed—and remember, this is merely what I've seen
during my own fish camp excursions—that there are typically a
good many cats outside of fish camp establishments. I don't know
why this troubles me, really, because I'm sure the cats are perfectly
lovely and purry and have many wonderful cat qualities, but on
some level I worry that there are two or seven cats on the premises
because they're needed to CATCH ALL THE RATS. I have no
proof of this, of course, and hopefully I'm totally off base. Maybe
those precious felines were just drawn to the smell of fish, much
like their kitty ancestors on the old Friskies cat-food commercials.

I'm sure that must be it.

But that still didn't stop me from eyeing a gray-and-white cat
with suspicion as David held open the screen door so we could
all walk inside.

Our supper that night was just as tasty and, well, *fried* as I had
hoped it would be. The fish was delicious, the hush puppies were
piping hot, and the sweet tea arrived in glasses that held at least
thirty-two ounces of fine Southern nectar. Everyone in attendance had a perfectly delightful time. But the fish camp, I guess
you could say, was really just the appetizer. The best part of the
night was still to come.

The ride home was pleasant but fairly uneventful. Joe experienced a pretty impressive memory surge around mile eight or nine—I believe we can attribute it to the miraculous powers of fish that has been battered and deep-fried in peanut oil—and he entertained us with stories about who used to live in that green house and where that old road used to lead before the highway opened in the early '70s. It was fun to hear him in such a lively mood, and when he'd occasionally trail off with an "Aw, dadgummit—I can't remember," we couldn't help but laugh. Chox often said that life with an Alzheimer's patient meant you had to do a lot of laughing to keep from crying, and she was right. There was too much heartache in the day to day, so those encounters with the funny felt like sunshine.

When you live several hours away from most of your family, there's really no sweeter blessing than having the luxury of just hanging out with them and traveling country roads and laughing and putting the hurt on some fried food as a family unit. As much as I love living in Birmingham, I can't help but miss my people; even though I've known them all my life, they continue to fascinate the fire out of me.

My mama, for example, is a Terribly Southern Woman. She does not go to the grocery store without having her hair coiffed, her makeup fixed, and her clothing ensemble perfectly coordinated. I was nineteen, in fact, before I saw her sit down for any extended period of time. For most of my life, she has been on her feet, cooking and cleaning and basically creating a warm and welcoming home for her husband and children. If she heard that your third cousin's niece had a death in her husband's family, she would bake them a pound cake.

Mama also has exceptional taste. As a child of the Depression, she knows how to do a lot with a little, and she's one of those people who are just drawn to the beautiful. Her Christmas tree decorating is legendary, and because she could give Job a run for his money in the patience department, she takes her time with everything she does. Thoughtful, intentional, meticulous—that's my mama, and anyone who knows her would tell you she's one of the most servant-hearted people they've ever met. If I called her right now and asked her to come to my house and shuck corn for three days (not that we do a whole lot of corn shuckin' around here, but I needed an example), she totally would. And on the off chance she needed a break from the corn duties, she'd relax by organizing my kitchen cabinets, straightening up my pantry, and looking around the house for anything that might need to go into the washing machine.

Oh, my word—I almost forgot to mention that part. Laundry is my mama's most favorite hobby. She'll wash two kitchen towels at a time just so the laundry fun will last all day long. Apparently I was absent on the day when the Lord distributed that particular piece of my DNA.

However, I have to admit that as Mama has crossed over into her sunset years, she has loosened up a bit, as well she should. She naps—sometimes for hours—in her chair. She'll stay in her (matching) pajamas for an entire day, and she's way more relaxed than she used to be, as evidenced by the fact that she now washes upwards of four kitchen towels at a time. Obviously she's a grandmother who likes to live on the edge.

Mama had an especially large time the night we went to the fish camp—she hooted and laughed all the way home. It reminded

me of when I was a little girl and would hear her on the telephone with one of her friends. She always listened more than she
talked, but when she got tickled—oh, my goodness. Her laugh—
sort of an "A-HOO! HOO! HOO!"—would pierce the silence
and make me grin from ear to ear.

By the time we pulled into Chox and Joe's driveway, it was
a little after ten. There had been a whole bunch of A-HOO!
HOO! HOO!-ing in the car, and I was a little sad that our big
night out was coming to an end. Joe was nineteen kinds of
thrilled about being home again, so he and Daddy immediately
unbuckled their seat belts and walked inside while David stayed
nearby to help Mama and Chox, who had been sitting in the
third row, get out of the car.

Navigating their way to a door required some doing, mainly
because they had to squeeze between the seats and then duck
down low enough to step out. Mama was first, with Chox right
behind her, and between the two of them they provided a veri-
table chorus of ailments within the span of about fifteen seconds.

"Oh! My shoulder is stiff. Hold on."

"Give me a minute. My back is sore."

"I can't go too fast. My toes are numb."

"Well, you don't even want to know how my elbow aches."

As we determined that the Battle of the Maladies was a draw,
Mama started laughing because she got sort of wedged between
the second row of seats and the door, with her behind way up in
the air. She reached out so David could help her, and while he
was grabbing her hand, he chuckled and said, "Are you gonna
make it, Ouida? Don't toot!" For some reason that struck our
collective funny bone, and all four of us started to laugh as David
pulled on Mama's arm to help her out of the truck.

The situation became increasingly hilarious with every passing second, with David tugging and Mama not making any real forward progress in terms of getting out of the truck, because in addition to being stuck, she was in stitches over the fact that her son-in-law had told her not to toot. The more she laughed, the more David pulled on her arm, and the more her behind crept higher in the air.

And listen. If I hadn't been there to witness it, I probably would've never believed it, but y'all, in the midst of all that laughter and silliness and good-time family fun, my mama, much to all of our surprise, hauled off and tooted. She surely did.

Right in her sister's face.

It was almost like David called it into being.

I would like to tell you that it was a very polite and delicate experience—that it was a mere whisper in the wind—but I cannot. No ma'am. Because the reality is that it was something akin to the sound of a freight train, or maybe even the freight train's blaring siren warning you to PLEASE GET OUT OF THE WAY before said train comes barreling through your home.

And if you thought we were laughing like crazy beforehand—well, it was full-blown hysteria afterward.

I could pretend that I giggled in a very ladylike fashion, but the fact of the matter is that I belly-laughed to the point that my bladder totally betrayed me. David had to sit down on Chox's retaining wall, and I thought he was going to quit breathing altogether—that's how hard he was gasping for air. Chox understandably scooted away from Mama and found a perch on the other side of the truck, holding her side while she tried to catch her breath.

Mama fell back in the car seat, and once she composed herself, she said, "WHEW! Oh, David, I've been holding that in the whole ride home! But like my mama always said, 'There's more room outside than there is inside! There's more room outside than inside!'"

About five minutes later, when we had ceased with the hyperventilating, David and I managed to say our good-byes so we could pick up Alex from Martha's house. David was barely capable of driving; he was still shaking with laughter. Crying, really.

And when I could pick up the words that were muffled beneath the laughter, here is what I heard:

"Thank you, God, for that. Oh, Lord, I needed that. Oh, God, thank you." And he wasn't just being funny. It was completely sincere gratitude to his Lord and Savior for blessing him with such a Special Gift during the Christmas season.

You should know that before I told this story I asked my mama's permission. I mean, heaven knows we all have gas skeletons in our closets, but I really didn't want to embarrass her.

So when I asked her if she minded my sharing the story, she hooted with laughter for a few seconds before she said, "No, I don't mind—I mean, I was just in such an awkward position trying to get out of that truck and I had been holding it and I just needed some RELIEF! That should tell you how comfortable I am around David. And do you know I think about that night all the time? I do! I think about it all the time!"

So do I, Mama.

So do I.

CHAPTER EIGHT

A Denominational Showdown in the Frozen Foods Aisle

ONE APRIL AFTERNOON I was sitting in Martha's living room, thumbing through the most recent issue of *Southern Living*, and she asked me if I'd tried a certain brand of frozen apple pie.

When I told her I hadn't, she explained why I should.

"Well," she began, "this kind that I'm telling you about has the Pippin apples. The Pippin apples! They're just so good and not too sweet, and you really do need to pick one up the next time you're at the Walmarts because they can be sort of hard to find.

"I mean, do you know—DO YOU KNOW," she continued, "that the last time our Walmarts got in a shipment of the Pippin pies, a friend of mine was there and she bought one and then she called me and she said, 'Martha, you have to get to Walmarts right now because they have a new shipment of Pippin pies.' So I put on some lipstick and hopped in my car and drove all the way to the Walmarts, and do you know—DO YOU KNOW,

SOPHIE—that some women from one of the Baptist churches had come in and bought every last one of those pies—every last one!—to serve at their Family Night Supper? They bought EVERY LAST ONE!

"So," she said with a laugh, "I hope you can find a Pippin pie at your Walmarts sometime soon because they surely are good. Not that I've had one recently or anything because, well, THE BAPTISTS GOT ALL OF OURS."

The end.

CHAPTER NINE

For Better, for Worse, and in the Increasingly Likely Chance of a Heatstroke

WHEN I WAS IN COLLEGE, I was pretty much the most selfish person in the universe. Oh, you can pat me on the back and tell me that I couldn't have been *that* bad, but I'm fairly certain I could have won a Miss Selfish Coed pageant, complete with a big ole crown, $200 in fanned-out cash money, and a complimentary sportswear competition evaluation by Mr. Greg, the Very Best Pageant Coach in northeastern Alabama/northwestern Georgia/ two smallish counties in southern Tennessee.

(I don't actually know a pageant coach named Mr. Greg.)

(But if I did, my guess is that we would bond immediately while he worked wonders with my hair and makeup.)

At the beginning of that particularly nasty run of self-centeredness that lasted from eighteen to twenty-five, some family friends of ours asked me to babysit. Robin and her husband, JD, were faithful members of my parents' church, where

Robin often moved the entire congregation to tears when she sang "Via Dolorosa." I thought she was a better singer than Sandi Patty even, and that is saying something considering I didn't think there was anything on earth more funky fresh than Sandi's rendition of "My God Is Real."

Remember when Sandi went up an octave at the end?

Chills.

I babysat a couple of times for Robin and JD's first child, a precious little boy named Bart, but I was so wrapped up in my senior year of high school that any babysitting gig was pretty much just a way for me to kill time until that blessed moment when I could get back in my car and ride around town in my 1981 Buick Century (yeah, I was pretty awesome) while I listened to either Amy Grant or Violent Femmes.

(Clearly I had very diverse musical tastes.)

(Or maybe I was in the midst of an identity crisis.)

(Or perhaps it was some combination of the two.)

A couple of months into my freshman year at Mississippi State, my mama called me with the news that Robin had given birth to a baby girl. We'd known since Robin was about two days pregnant that she was going to name a girl Mae, and that's precisely what she did. Little Mae was an absolutely gorgeous baby—all blonde hair and blue eyes and sweet little smocked dresses—and when I went home for Christmas that winter, I babysat Bart and his new baby sister for several days in a row. By day two I was absolutely smitten; even now I tell Mae that she was the first baby I ever loved. That little ten-pound bundle made me wonder for a split second if I might just be able to put another person's needs in front of my own someday, and for an eighteen-year-old, self-absorbed fool (FOOL, I SAY VERILY UNTO YOU), that was a new and different line of thinking. I was still miles away from Thoughts of Motherhood, but at least it was a baby step toward selflessness, so to speak.

Since Robin owned a clothing store in my hometown, she had a flexible but busy career, and at some point in the spring of my sophomore year—when Mae was officially into the toddler stage and Robin was officially back in the swing of being a working mama—Robin asked if I'd like to babysit Bart and Mae during my summer break. The prospect of keeping those darling young'uns for three whole months was more than I could resist, so I agreed. And lest you marvel at my maturity, you should know that there were three primary motivating factors in my decision: (1) since Robin owned a clothing store, I hoped beyond all hope that she would pay me in sassy new outfits; (2) Mae was just learning to work the big bow into her hairstyle repertoire, and while I was not good for much in the way of discipleship at that stage in my life, I was highly qualified to be a little girl's big-bow mentor; and (3) I'm not sure if I mentioned this, but since Robin owned a clothing store, I hoped beyond all hope that she would pay me in sassy new outfits.

What can I say? I was a simple girl with simple needs.

Plus, I *really* needed some new 100-percent-wool outfits to wear to Mississippi State football games that September. Because even if the thermometer said eighty-five degrees, the calendar said, OH, YES, MA'AM, IT IS FALL, and I wouldn't have dreamed of not adhering to the seasonal fashion codes.

Really, I was a wellspring of sense and substance. Yes, I was.

Much to my surprise, my summer with "the children" turned out to be pretty idyllic, even though the daily responsibilities of looking after a five-year-old and a one-year-old required me to demonstrate some responsibility by doing things like "waking up on time" and "feeding the little people" and "following through with commitments." Mae initially had a little trouble saying my name—the *ph* sound gave her fits—but by the second week of summer, that precious twenty-month-old had figured out a name for me that sidestepped the pesky digraph: "MAMA SOAKIE? MAAAAA-MA SOOOOOOAK-IEEEE!"

I'll never forget where I was standing the first time I heard her say it. I was at the breakfast bar, fixing Bart something to drink, and from that moment on, I was officially toast—toast that was wrapped around Mae's tiny index finger, I might add. The entire summer became an exercise in Indulging the Children. Bart and I played Nintendo, Mae and I sang all the songs from the *Stealing Home* sound track (she and Bart liked to break out their best dance moves to "Great Balls of Fire"), and I carted them all over town just like they were my own.

It's hard to explain unless you were, you know, *me* during that time, but in lots of ways babysitting Bart and Mae gave me a purpose when I didn't really feel like I had one. I mean, I guess technically the fact that I was in charge of planning the Chi Omega Choo-Choo party for fall rush should have given me some sort of purpose, but as you might imagine, basing one's identity on sorority party planning is sort of a risky proposition. I believe that's what the experts might refer to as *shaky psychological ground*.

My renewed sense of purpose wasn't the only benefit to spending my summer with a couple of adorable kids, though. Lots of afternoons Robin and I would visit when she got home from work, and I was always astounded by the way she talked about Jesus. He was such an integral part of her life that she talked about Him like she would talk about a friend (a supremely holy friend, mind you, but a friend just the same), and even though in my head I could relate to how openly she shared her faith, I remember feeling like a piece of the Jesus puzzle must be missing from my heart. I'd trusted in Christ for salvation at a church camp when I was in ninth grade (Did you notice my Reformed-ish language just then? Thank you. Thank you so much. I believe John Calvin would be proud of me despite the fact that my life has been the denominational equivalent of Heinz 57), and a few years later, when I was a senior in high school, there was an emotional rededication of my life at another church camp. However, I have to admit that the rededication may have been prompted more by lingering guilt over the illicit consumption of some Bartles & Jaymes wine coolers a few weeks prior than by any real work of the Holy Spirit.

Perhaps you've picked up on the fact that I was walking around with some rock-solid theology during that particular period of my life.

The bottom line is that, by the time I got to college, I had full confidence that I was a believer, but what I didn't have was any spiritual maturity. I kept waiting for Jesus to just fix everything that was wrong with me, and when He didn't, I wondered if I'd missed some critical step along the way, if maybe I'd missed church on the day when somebody explained how that "following Jesus stuff" worked once the mountaintop experience of youth retreat was over.

Robin, on the other hand, seemed totally committed to walking out her faith on a daily basis. She loved (and still loves, I might add) the Lord with sincere transparency, and it fascinated me. Over and over again I wanted to ask her how she and Jesus had made it from point A to point B, but my pride wouldn't let me. That tendency to pretend I had stuff all figured out when I actually didn't have the foggiest idea what was going on was one of my most consistent weaknesses during my teens and twenties, and WHOA, NELLIE OLESON, did I ever pay the price for that again and again, especially in my walk with the Lord.

So for the rest of that pre-junior-year summer—and throughout the rest of my college days, in fact—Robin, JD, Bart, and Mae were a big part of my life. We'd eat supper together at Mama and Daddy's house when I was home on weekends, we'd visit when they were in Starkville for a football game, and they became a very real extension of my family. When I flirted with going off the deep end during my second year of grad school and for a few years that followed (I basically decided to question everything I'd ever professed to believe and, while I was at it, say a big, fat "NO, THANK YOU" to anyone who tried to step into my life with some wisdom), they continued to love me. It couldn't have been easy.

Even though those years weren't my favorites, and even though I made some choices that, as Sister would say, pretty much make me want to claw off my face when I think about them, I always kept a little picture of Bart and Mae on my nightstand. In some small way I think I felt responsible to them. The picture, which is in the playroom off my kitchen right this very second, was from that first summer when I babysat the kids every day, and it was a reminder of a time that was far happier and far better than the awkward, angst-filled years of my early twenties that followed.

To be fair, there were also some really good times in my early twenties. It's just that in retrospect, I think there may have been some moderate, albeit undiagnosed, "HEY, MAMA SOAKIE, IT MIGHT BE WISE TO CONSULT WITH A PROFESSIONAL" depression going on. So for better or for worse, I tend to remember the dark more than I remember the light. And certainly more than I remember the Light.

Eventually I grew out of my early-twenties identity crisis and my annoying tendency to shirk responsibility. I got engaged, got married, found a life-changing job, moved to Birmingham, found another life-changing job, joined a wonderful church, learned to navigate the inevitable hurdles of life without plunging into a melodramatic crisis of faith, etc., and so forth, amen. I also became a mama, and by the time that happened, Bart and Mae were nineteen and fifteen, respectively. They were both growing up to be what my daddy would call Really Fine People, and I have to say that seeing the two of them hold Alex for the first time is one of my favorite mama memories—which is why I have approximately 481 pictures to document that momentous occasion. I remember looking at Alex, who was about three months old, then looking at them and thinking, *Okay. Robin and JD managed to get Bart and Mae to the point where they no longer cry incessantly, they feed themselves, and they sleep through the night. I CAN TOTALLY DO THIS.*

By the time Alex was five (and I certainly don't mean to brag, but he was potty trained and everything, y'all), Bart and Mae were bona fide grown-ups. Both of them worked for their family's business, and when I couldn't keep up with the state of their respective dating lives by asking them seventy-eight questions and embarrassing the fire out of them in person, I'd go with the next best option and ask Mama to fill me in whenever we talked on the phone. My just-ask-Mama system worked beautifully for several years, and it was sometime in late 2008, if memory serves, when Mama told me that Mae was dating someone new. Since I don't think that there's any such thing as too much information, I tried to get as many details from Mama as possible.

"Well," I demanded, "who is he?"

"He's *such* a nice boy. He's from south Mississippi, graduated from Mississippi College, and I think—I *really do think*—that she's just crazy about him," Mama answered.

I was intrigued, so I continued with the interrogation. "What do Robin and JD think? Do they like him? Is it serious?"

"Oh, they're crazy about him too. And I don't know if it's serious yet, but I think it will be."

I had to pause for a second and process what I was hearing. In my head Mae would forever be every bit of three years old and twirling around her parents' sunroom in a ruffled, polka-dot romper. The very notion that she could be in a potentially serious relationship 'bout near overloaded my circuitry. I snapped back to reality, though, when I realized that I'd failed to ask a very important question.

"Mama! I almost forgot! What's his name?"

"Scoot!"

"What? You want me to scoot? Scoot where? Can't I just walk?" I asked.

"Noooo, honey." Mama sounded just a little bit exasperated. "I was talking about Mae's new boyfriend. His *name* is Scoot."

"His name is *Scoot?*"

"Yes!" At that point Mama's tone indicated that she didn't quite understand why I was struggling to process such a simple piece of information. "It's Scoot! Scoot is his name! That's what I'm telling you!"

Now, listen. I recognize that I am the product of a family that shouldn't throw a single name-related stone. But Scoot was a new one for me. It struck me as a more memorable moniker than Sister's friend Edna Earl (Sister called her Ed for short). It might even top a distant cousin whose name was Stellawood, but we'd have to put it to a vote to decide for sure.

It wasn't long before Scoot was like part of our big ole

extended family. Mama made sure to let me know he was "going to make a doctor"—which is Moss Rose speak for "he's currently enrolled in medical school"—and in Mama's book, the combination of his honorable career path, his love for the Lord, and his love for Mae catapulted him to Favored Among Men status in record time. He proposed to Mae in October, and in Myrtlewood, Mississippi, that means that within two hours of Mae saying yes, wedding plans were moving full steam ahead.

I don't know if other small towns operate the same way, but Myrtlewood folks aren't real big on wasting time where event planning is concerned. In fact, I'm fully convinced that the nation's largest concentration of out-of-this-world hostesses and party givers resides within the confines of my home county. There must be a chemical in the water there that imparts extensive knowledge of table settings, floral design, and cooking for a crowd. Beats anything I've ever seen.

By Christmas Robin and Mae had the bulk of the wedding plans figured out. The wedding was going to be outside at Robin and JD's home, and when Mama told me that Mae was going to get married in the backyard of the house where she'd grown up, my first question was, "So, what all is Robin going to do when she remodels her house?" I'm sure my reaction might seem odd to some people, but by the time I was ten or eleven, I'd learned that if a woman offered on a Monday to host a bridal tea, baby shower, or wedding reception, her first task on Tuesday morning was to line up a contractor. It wasn't that she was trying to outdo anyone else; it was just that hosting a big event was the perfect opportunity to force her husband's hand if he'd been putting off a home-improvement project.

For example.

When I was growing up, we had stone pavers leading to our

front door. Those pavers were notorious for being a little on the wobbly side and tricky to navigate in heels. Nonetheless, they served as the walkway through our front yard for years. But after Mama offered to host a bridal tea for our church's organist? Oh, those pavers were history. Within four days, Mama had scheduled a cement truck to pour her a new walkway. After all, how in the world could she risk Virginia Peterson's heel getting caught in the grass? Or what if Barbara Riley tripped trying to step from paver to paver? Or what if Fleta Mears slid on a mossy spot and dropped her gift and the bride-to-be would never be able to serve her own guests with that cream-and-sugar set in Lenox Solitaire? That wouldn't be very Christlike, now, would it?

So when Robin decided to tweak a few spaces around her house for the wedding, she was really just following in the footsteps of countless Mississippi women who had gone before her. With the help of a mighty fine architect and some hardworking contractors, she fine-tuned the landscaping in her yard and added a few hardscape features, which is my fancy way of telling you she had her contractor build an outdoor fireplace as well as a beautiful altar area where Mae and Scoot would say their vows. She also extended an enclosed porch that ran along the back of the house so it could accommodate more people. By the time spring gave way to summer that year, Robin and JD's home looked like something straight out of *Southern Living*. It was going to be an absolutely perfect setting for a June wedding.

I spent most of Mae's wedding week in Myrtlewood, and on the actual day of the wedding, I woke up pretty early so that Alex and I could be ready for pictures at eight. He and five of his cousins were in the wedding party, and I was counting on

Brother to be able to tie the boys' bow ties. Since I'm pretty sure you can minor in bow tying at Ole Miss, I expected Brother to be highly qualified.

The morning was muggy, with an unseasonably heavy haze hanging in the air, and when I broke into a sweat just trying to get Alex, me, and all our stuff loaded in the car at seven forty-five in the morning, I wondered how the rest of the day was going to pan out. Resolved that a little humidity wasn't going to ruin the day, I cranked up the AC in my car, spackled a little more powder on my face, and hit the road.

Over the course of my life I've witnessed way more than my fair share of beautiful Southern nuptials, but I have to say my first glimpse of Robin and JD's yard completely took my breath away. I don't know if I've seen a lovelier setting for a wedding. The bride and her mother had thought of every detail, including monogrammed fans wrapped in coordinating ribbon, as well as a lemonade table at the entrance to the backyard so guests could enjoy a cool drink as they found their seats. Hydrangeas were in full bloom in the flower beds, while ceramic and stone planters overflowed with roses, caladiums, daisies, and impatiens. Tables covered in green silk dotted the periphery of the yard, and enormous glass containers of sweet tea and ice water took the place of the traditional punch bowl. JD's classic (read: ancient) pickup truck was parked under the trees so that the truck bed, which was covered with quilts and flanked by urns of knockout roses, could accommodate a homemade ice cream buffet after the ceremony.

If love is in the details—well, the world could barely contain all the love at Robin and JD's house that morning.

By eight thirty, picture taking was going full force, and I noticed that the sun felt unusually, um, *aggressive* for that time of the day. Paige and I focused on keeping the kids happy and well hydrated, and by nine o'clock the musicians—including a full gospel choir—had taken their places in the shade and started to warm up. Around nine fifteen I decided to take a quick stroll, mainly to soak in the sight of all those flowers one more time, but the sun was so relentless that I lasted for two whole minutes before I hightailed it back inside. I filled up a Solo cup with ice water faster than you can say, "High potential for dangerous UV rays," and I braced myself for what was shaping up to be a humdinger of a scorcher.

Regardless of what was going on with the heat index (my conservative estimation: 162 degrees), the bride was cool as a cucumber. She looked the way every girl dreams of looking on her wedding day: elegant, happy, and serene. Paige's three-year-old was mopping sweat off his forehead after picture time, mind you, but not Mae. She glowed, but she never glistened. I know with everything in me that if I had married under the same weather conditions, someone would have had to follow me around with an assortment of towels, a vat of loose powder, and a block of ice, but Mae required none of the above. Inexplicably, she was not sweating at all. And as I lifted my hair off my neck and looked around for the ministry of the nearest air-conditioning vent, I tried my best not to resent her for that.

A quick preceremony survey of the backyard revealed that there wasn't a folding chair to spare at T minus 15 minutes, and a couple of hundred people were standing in a semicircle in the area behind the chairs. My sister-in-law Janie and I claimed a couple of patio chairs next to the outdoor fireplace, mainly because we felt it was wise to be near our boys when they lined up for the processional. We expected that they'd behave, but we figured proximity would be to our advantage, especially in the event that a well-timed "STOP THAT. STOP THAT RIGHT NOW" glare proved necessary.

The children were definitely fidgety, but they did remarkably well considering the stifling humidity. Most of the men in attendance had abandoned their coats and loosened their ties; the backs of their shirts looked like damp pastel dartboards. The ribbon-covered fans were getting a workout, but unfortunately it's difficult to create a breeze when you're in the dead center of a stifling heat vortex. Janie and I fanned ourselves like we were getting paid for it and thanked the good Lord the sun was tucked behind a pretty large cloud cover. Because that cloud cover? Well, it was pretty much the only thing standing between us and a heatstroke.

A few minutes after ten, someone opened the French doors that led to the patio, and Mae floated down the steps with Robin on one side and JD on the other. I've never been big on princesses and fairy tales and the like, but even I'll admit that the only thing missing on Mae's wedding day was a glass slipper and a carriage. She was stunning. And as she walked down the aisle with her head held high and her hand resting on her daddy's arm, the sun peeked from behind the clouds and followed her like a spotlight. It was like the Lord Himself was shining on Mae and Scoot as they prepared to say their vows and spend the rest of their lives together.

I dabbed the edges of my forehead in a futile attempt to keep the sweat from running down my face, and as the minister was about to lead all of us in prayer, I bowed my head a few seconds early and offered up a prayer of my own: *Lord, it's real sweet and all that You made the sun very literally shine on them on their wedding day. You really do think of everything. But if You could tuck that sun back behind those clouds for the rest of the ceremony, I'd be sixteen kinds of grateful. Because it would make this day extra special if I didn't have to fight off a bout of the sun poisoning. In Jesus' name.*

See, here's the thing. On any given day, I can easily rattle off a list of the Top Ten Most Blazing Hot Moments of My Life. When I was a freshman in college, there was an unfortunate encounter with a tanning bed that left me stretched across the tile floor of my dorm bathroom with an inch-thick coating of Noxzema all over my stomach and legs. In the early '90s there was a trip to New Orleans for my friend Elise's bachelorette party, and the air was so stale and thick and steamy that I nearly had to seek counseling in order to overcome my heat-related resentment. Just recently there was a sweltering canoe ride in Ecuador that culminated with a climb up a fairly intimidating number of steps and the sobering realization that the nearest breeze was obviously trapped somewhere along the southern coast of Chile.

So when that sun came out—and stayed out, I might add—at Mae's wedding, it got my attention, and fast. It was blazing. Epic. Brutal. Right up there on my HOTTEST MOMENTS EVER list, sandwiched somewhere between Elise's bachelorette party and the Ecuadorian jungle. That sun showed up with some authority.

Janie and I tried our best to be gamers as we continued to fan ourselves at a pace that would impress the most hyperactive dragonfly, but when I started to feel my scalp burn, I very discreetly stood up from my wrought-iron chair, pulled my dress away from the backs of my legs, then ever so slowly tiptoed to the back door. I gently turned the knob as I pushed on the side panel, and the blast of cold air that hit me straight in the face prompted a spontaneous outpouring of thanksgiving and praise. I've spent most of my life steeped in a deeply traditional Protestant church culture, but that day? When my sizzling scalp and I encountered the sweet relief of an indoor environment where the thermostat was set to a brisk sixty-two degrees? I may have spoken in tongues.

Unfortunately, the heat outside got worse before it got better. Brother and I ended up watching the ceremony through a den window, and Brother took it upon himself to serve as my personal wedding commentator for the remainder of the festivities.

"We've got a lady in yellow who's down for the count on the back row," he'd say, and sure enough, the lady in yellow would stand up and make her way inside.

"I don't think Robin's cousin from Charlotte is going to be able to take much more," he'd predict, and within minutes we'd hear a hearty "WHEWWWWWW" as the cousin walked in the back door and made a beeline for a glass of ice water.

The commentating highlight of the day was when Brother gestured to the right side of the yard and said, "Hey, look over there. I'm pretty sure one of the people in the choir just vomited."

I didn't believe him at first, but his play-by-play skills were dead on. After some friends helped the choir member inside and she cooled down a little, she was as good as new, but the heat was definitely taking a toll. I wouldn't go so far as to say that people were dropping like flies, but I would say they were beginning to drop like widely spaced dominoes.

The bride, however, remained perfectly radiant. And once she and Scoot were pronounced husband and wife, the collective sum of their happiness rendered the heat all but meaningless. The pastor said the benediction, which meant everyone was free and clear to put the smackdown on some iced tea. I saw some of the most refined women I have ever known slam their glasses of iced tea like they were fraternity boys playing a heated game

of beer pong, and the ladies who were really living on the edge
followed up that glass of iced tea with a glass of fresh lemonade.
SOUTHERN WOMEN GONE WILD.

During the reception my little family and I found a spot
underneath a great big pine tree, and Alex quickly untucked
his shirt and removed his bow tie while his daddy fixed them a
couple of plates of food. The menu of honey-glazed pork tenderloin, green beans, sweet potato fries, fried chicken, and cheese
grits was enough to make Paula Deen weep with joy, and as the
little man dug into his "deeeee-licious" plate of cheese grits, I
spotted Martha, who was stylishly sporting a long-sleeved black
jacket in the aforementioned 162-degree heat. She looked like
she had just stepped away from the Estée Lauder counter (after
a quick stop by the beauty parlor to get her hair shampooed and
styled, of course), and as I tucked my lifeless, humidity-riddled
hair behind my ears and wiped the sweat from my nose, I may
have harbored some significant resentment toward my mother-
in-law in that moment. She looked fresh as a daisy, and I looked
like I'd thrown on a dress in the car after finishing the ten-to-four
shift on the highway repaving crew.

NOT THAT I WAS BITTER.

After I'd made my peace with the fact that I looked like I'd
run a half marathon even though I'd just been, you know, *standing*, I very deliberately let my eyes wander around the whole
expanse of the yard. I looked to my right and saw my third
grade teacher and her beautiful daughter, who'd recently gotten engaged. Straight ahead my cousin Benji was laughing like
crazy with his two daughters. Mama's cousins Jean and Judy
were standing to my left, talking and carrying on with Alex, and
as I turned around, I caught a glimpse of Bart helping a lady to
her car way off in the distance. Mama, who was rivaling Martha

in the "Oh, is it hot? I hadn't noticed" department, was right behind me, telling Robin's mother what a glorious morning it had been. And then, as I turned back to my original position, I spotted Chox with Minnie, her dear friend of more than forty years, standing at the edge of the driveway, no doubt making supper plans for later that night.

It was several minutes before I was able to mentally assemble the puzzle pieces of what I'd just seen, but eventually it dawned on me: *I was surrounded on all sides by people I'd known and loved for years.* Maybe that doesn't resonate with you the way it resonates with me, but even now it's a powerful visual reminder—at least to me—that God doesn't just touch down in our lives for short periods of time and then take off when He's ready for a new adventure. He sets up camp. Puts up fences. Establishes boundary lines in pleasant places. And then He surrounds us with people who do their very best to make sure we don't wander too far from the fold.

Standing in Robin and JD's yard, I was reminded of all those days when I babysat Bart and Mae, those times when I went through the churchy motions but struggled to articulate what I believed, much less why I believed it. I had wondered if I'd ever get married, if I'd ever want to be a mama, if I'd ever feel comfortable in my own skin. And as I stood in front of the house where I'd wrestled with so much internal questioning in my late teens and early twenties, I grinned just a little bit and thought, *Well, my word. What a difference twenty years makes. I'm surrounded by the same people, but by the grace of God, I have a completely different perspective.*

I don't know. It's weird. But sometimes the Lord has to take us back to a place we've been so He can remind us just how far we've come.

There's a passage in the Psalms I absolutely love—I'm convinced it will resonate way down deep in my heart as long as I live. And if there were some way the forty-two-year-old version of me could travel back in time, sit down, and visit with twenty-two-year-old me, I would hand that twenty-two-year-old a little slip of paper with Psalm 107:4-8 printed on it. Well, first I would tell her to wash her face every single night and moisturize like crazy even though she can't fathom a day when her pores will be visible. But after we'd addressed skin-care issues, I'd read her these verses:

> Some of you wandered for years in the desert,
>   looking but not finding a good place to live,
> Half-starved and parched with thirst,
>   staggering and stumbling, on the brink of exhaustion.
> Then, in your desperate condition, you called out to GOD.
>   He got you out in the nick of time;
> He put your feet on a wonderful road
>   that took you straight to a good place to live.
> So thank GOD for his marvelous love,
>   for his miracle mercy to the children he loves.

(That's *The Message* translation, by the way.)

(And I think it's important for all of us to acknowledge that whenever we quote a passage from *The Message*, the ESV totally rolls its eyes.)

I think I'd give twenty-two-year-old me a great big hug, and then I would gently grab her by the shoulders, look her straight in the eyes, and say, "Hey. You know when you used to go to church all the time and you sang that hymn called 'Great Is Thy

Faithfulness'? Remember that, sister. Because God is going to continue to prove Himself faithful in your life. And one day, when you're at Mae's wedding reception (Side note: she marries a guy named Scoot. SCOOT! Isn't that fun?), you really will know who you are. But more important, you will know Whose you are. And you will marvel at the countless ways that you've seen the goodness of the Lord in the land of the living.

"So go ahead and embrace the inevitable. No matter how hard you try to run, He's not going to give up on you. He's not. You can take that to the spiritual bank, my friend. And unlike your regular bank, your account at the spiritual bank is not currently overdrawn because of that check you wrote at the Starkville B-Quik for $2.94 worth of potato logs.

"But that's probably another discussion for another time."

CHAPTER TEN

Lordy, Lordy, Look Who's One Hundred-y

ON SISSIE'S ONE HUNDREDTH BIRTHDAY, we celebrated with a luncheon at Martha's house. Martha had recently relocated to a new patio home after selling the place where she'd lived for more than forty years, and by the time Sissie's birthday rolled around, the family, I'm happy to say, was almost fully recovered from the Moving Martha project. There's probably no need to share all the Moving Martha details—and besides, if I did, I'm pretty sure YOUR HEAD WOULD EXPLODE.

Suffice it to say that after David's brother, Scott, and sister-in-law, Rose, had worked tirelessly to get the details of the real-estate transactions squared away, the actual move started with Martha asking David if he could install a phone line in her new garage—HER GARAGE—and ended with Martha asking me to make phone calls about a four-piece wrought-iron patio set from Target, a stepladder from Home Depot (but not with wide steps! not with wide steps!), and a large, two-door Rubbermaid storage container that "you can buy for less than $80! It's less than $80!"

David would tell you that the Moving Martha experience changed him in ways he will never be able to articulate. He would also tell you that he need never hear the word *sconces* again.

Precious family memories, people. Precious family memories.

Since Sissie was living in a nursing home when she turned the big 1-0-0, we initially thought that we'd have to go there to throw her birthday party. But over the course of that spring her health improved, and we were thrilled when the head nurse gave her the go-ahead to spend her birthday at Martha's. That Sunday morning David and Scott went to the nursing home to pick up the birthday girl, and I couldn't help but picture the three of them ditching the party and heading off on some sort of *Cannonball Run*-ish road race. You know the drill. David and Scott would trail for three-quarters of the race, and at the last minute Sissie would knock one of them out of the driver's seat, take command of the wheel, and then lead them to a stunning come-from-behind victory.

Apparently the subpar comedies of the early 1980s left a deep and lasting legacy in my heart.

I'm looking at you, *Rhinestone*.

Fortunately Sissie made it to Martha's without staging a vehicular coup in order to overtake Burt Reynolds and Dom DeLuise, and her hair held up just beautifully in the six whole minutes it had to endure the wind and humidity. Once they were all inside the house, David and Scott moved Sissie, who was in her wheelchair, to the dining room, and the rest of us took turns telling Sissie happy birthday. Martha was concerned that Sissie wouldn't be able to see or hear the person talking to her, so whenever someone would speak to Sissie, Martha would say something along the lines of "YOU HAVE TO YELL A LITTLE! YOU HAVE TO YELL A LITTLE! HOLD ON! I'LL TELL HER!"

And then: "MOTHER! IT'S ROSE! IT'S ROSE! AND SHE'S HERE FOR YOUR BIRTHDAY!"

My personal favorite moment was when my mama walked over to Sissie, leaned over, grabbed her hand, and said, "Sissie? This is Ouida. Happy birthday!"

And then Sissie said, "RITA?"

And Mama said, "No, it's Ouida."

And Sissie said, "RITA?!"

And Martha said, "YOU HAVE TO YELL! YOU HAVE TO YELL!"

And Mama said, "IT'S NOT RITA. IT'S OUIDA!"

And Sissie said, "Oh. Hey, Ouida. How are you?"

A few minutes later I asked Martha if I could take her picture with Sissie, and she said, "Oh, yes! Oh, yes! But just keep in mind that this isn't my real jacket; it's my cooking jacket. It's just my cooking jacket!"

I'll bet you a dollar to a donut that Martha's cooking jacket came from the Stein Mart petites' department. And as a brief side note, I would just like to ask you to please take a moment to really absorb the fact that my mother-in-law owns a jacket that is *specifically reserved for cooking*.

Thank you. Your life will be all the better for it.

The birthday meal was sort of a late brunch, which I guess you'd just call, you know, *lunch,* but we had brunchy food: breakfast casserole, hash brown casserole, fresh fruit, rolls, birthday cake, and ice cream. We also had a pineapple-and-apple casserole that Martha had bought at her church's fall festival and then put in the freezer, but she was sixteen kinds of nervous about serving it since she didn't know who had made it. The situation made me laugh because, well, there are always two or three people of questionable culinary ability in every congregation, and there's no doubt in my

mind that if I had thrown out one of those iffy names as the hypothetical chef, Martha would have dumped that casserole down the
disposal and never looked back.

You can't be too careful! You just can't be too careful!

A few minutes before we sat down at the table, Rose and I
were putting ice in the glasses when Sissie very suddenly yelled,
"HELP! HELP!" and nearly scared us to death. Fortunately she
was sitting only about six inches away from us, so Rose leaned
over and said, "Sissie? Is everything okay?"

"Oh, everything's fine," Sissie answered. "I just wanted to
make sure y'all remembered I'm here."

Sissie yelled, "HELP! HELP!" one more time during lunch,
and again, it was just to make sure we were giving her the attention she deserved. She had no cause for concern, though. I think
on some level every one of us knew it was the last time we'd
share a meal with Sissie sitting at the head of the table, and we
all wanted to give the day the honor it was due. It was incredibly
touching to see Martha's dining room chairs filled with four generations of family, to sit back and take in the fact that there was a
ninety-four-year gap between the oldest and the youngest person
present. Every once in a while the six-year-old, Alex, would pop
out of his chair to give the one-hundred-year-old a hug and a
few pats on the shoulder, and it was a gift—*a gift*—to see them
together. I didn't know my great-grandparents, so I'm extra grateful that Alex understands the joy of not only knowing his great-
grandmother but also adoring her—and having full confidence
that the feeling is entirely mutual.

After lunch Sissie topped off her meal with several huge scoops
of Blue Bell Homemade Vanilla ice cream. Rose and I kept waiting for Sissie to say that she'd had enough, but she'd finish one
scoop and immediately ask for another. I think it must be all kinds

of wonderful to celebrate your centennial birthday and enjoy a bottomless bowl of ice cream while your daughter, grandsons, granddaughters-in-law, and great-grandchildren remind you how much they treasure and love you. That has to be one of those "blessings all mine, with ten thousand beside" moments, you know?

Once Sissie polished off the last of her ice cream, we all wanted to take a few more pictures with the birthday girl. Martha mentioned that she had a little something for Sissie in the next room, so Rose and I adjusted Sissie's jacket while Martha assured us, "This will only take a second! Just a second! But I just have to have it! Have to have it!" as she walked down the hallway.

Martha was holding a nosegay of hot-pink roses when she came back to the dining room, and as she handed it to Sissie, she leaned down right next to Sissie's ear, and in her most gentle whisper-scream, she said, "Mother? Mother? These flowers are for you, sugar. They're for you! Now hold these flowers, Mother! Hold these pretty flowers! Hold these flowers and let us take your pretty picture! Pretty picture!"

Rose and I were a little puzzled about why the flowers were such a big deal to Martha. They were a thoughtful gesture, and they definitely matched Sissie's hot-pink jacket, but Martha's enthusiasm for the flowers was off the charts. Right about the time I was going to ask why the flowers were of such Critical Picture-Related Importance, Martha started talking to Sissie again.

"Hold the flowers, Mother! Turn them just a little bit toward me! Oh, that's perfect, sugar! Just perfect! I want you to have your flowers so we can take your picture and put it in *The Myrtlewood Tribune* and everybody will see my beautiful mother holding those beautiful flowers! Every beautiful mother needs some beautiful flowers! And you are—well, you are just the sweetest mother in the whole wide world! The sweetest and most beautiful mother!"

When Martha finished her explanation, Sissie looked up at her with the faintest glimmer of tears in her eyes, and she smiled. In that moment, those two were a living, breathing portrait of the sometimes ineffable affection between a mother and her child.

And Martha was right. Sissie was, at least in our family's opinion, the sweetest and most beautiful one-hundred-year-old to ever grace the pages of *The Myrtlewood Tribune*. She established a legacy that will ripple for generations, and she didn't have to yell, "HELP! HELP!" at her birthday luncheon to remind us of that.

We knew it then.

We know it now.

And we will never, ever forget it.

CHAPTER ELEVEN

When Prayer Meeting Includes a Cocktail Hour

ONE OF THE HIGHLIGHTS of every summer is our annual beach trip with the cousins, a tradition that actually started by accident. When Alex was five, our little family happened to be at Scott and Rose's beach condo the same time that Chox, Joe, Benji, Paige, and their families were at a condo a few miles down the road. After hanging out together for a few days and sharing meals and watching the little cousins play nonstop in the pool, we thought, *Well, this is pretty much a genius idea. We should get together like this more often.*

So we do. We find a week during the summer that works for as many of us as possible, and we go to the beach together. We even stay in the same condo—we feel like the kids make more memories that way—and even though it can get crowded and sleep becomes a precious commodity and we honest-to-goodness look like the Clampetts when we pull in the parking lot with a week's worth of luggage and pool toys and groceries stuffed in our cars, the trip has become our version of a family reunion. We cook and eat and laugh and swim and sun and then laugh some more. It's big fun.

Joe was a few years into his battle with Alzheimer's when we started the beach trip tradition, and his absolute top priority was to be wherever Chox was, even if that meant he had to be away from home for a few days. Chox and Paige would spend most of the drive from Myrtlewood to Mobile answering Joe's questions about where they were going, but eventually—usually around the time that he caught his first glimpse of Mobile Bay—he'd sit back, relax, and enjoy the ride.

Once everybody arrived in Orange Beach and Paige and I started the elaborate unpacking process, Joe liked to sit on our condo's balcony and look out at the Gulf. He'd always loved the beach, and he'd stay out on that balcony all day if we let him. I think the sight of all that water must have been a comfort to him in the midst of otherwise unfamiliar surroundings.

Water always looks like water, you know? No matter where you are.

Joe had long relished the familiar, even before the Alzheimer's started to take hold. Over the course of their marriage, Chox and Joe built some deep, lasting friendships with ten or twelve other couples in Myrtlewood, and for the better part of twenty years, one of their favorite things to do with those friends was to meet on Wednesday nights for supper at the country club. They'd initially gather at the bar for a glass of wine or a margarita, and then they'd commandeer the biggest table in the dining room so they could share a meal and catch up on the latest news in everybody's lives. Since most of the folks in their group were Methodist or Episcopalian, they didn't have Wednesday night church obligations like the Baptists did, so Joe jokingly started to refer to their meals together as their own personal "Prayer Meeting." The name stuck, and if Chox and Joe ever mentioned that they were headed to Prayer Meeting on a Wednesday night, we all knew that we could find them at the country club.

The Lord can meet us anywhere, you know.

I tell you all that because on our second annual beach trip, Joe had Prayer Meeting on the brain. He told Chox over and over again that he wanted to make sure they were back in Myrtlewood in time for Prayer Meeting, and by the way, what day was it? And did they need to go ahead and leave for Prayer Meeting? And had she checked with the folks from Prayer Meeting? And was Prayer Meeting still on Wednesdays? And were their friends expecting them at Prayer Meeting? Because he *really* wanted to be at Prayer Meeting.

If you had overheard him without knowing that he was in the throes of Alzheimer's, you probably would've thought he was the most devout man you'd ever met. You might have called him Reverend, even. Or at the very least assumed he was an elder.

And listen. That would've tickled him to no end.

In addition to the Prayer Meeting obsession, Joe also had a tough time finding his way around the condo that year. There were several times that first afternoon (and night) when he'd announce that he needed to go to the restroom, and instead of turning left to go into his and Chox's room, he'd invariably head down the hallway past the kitchen, then turn to go in the room where Paige and her family were staying. Chox would chase behind him, saying, "No, Joe! Not that way! Come this way!" He'd finally turn around, mumble something under his breath, shrug his shoulders, and follow her.

And then, after a few seconds: "Chox? When are we going to Prayer Meeting?"

"Not right now, Joe. We're at the beach, remember?" she'd calmly reply. And for a little while, at least, that answer would satisfy him.

The first night of our trip proved interesting. Since Joe tended to get up and fix himself a late-night/early-morning snack when he was at home, Chox and Paige anticipated that Joe might be prone to some nocturnal wanderings at the condo, too. They were a little fearful he might go out on the balcony and not remember how to get back inside, so they made sure to fasten the child latch on the sliding glass door before Joe turned in for the night. And even though the front door was heavy and extremely difficult to open, Paige flipped every available lock and lever. Just to be safe.

Sure enough, Joe made his way to the kitchen sometime after midnight. Chox left his usual snack on the kitchen counter so he wouldn't rummage through cabinets and drawers, and after he'd polished off his Little Debbie Nutty Bar and half a can of Coke (or Co-Cola, as he called it), he turned to go back to the bedroom.

But somewhere along the way, he lost his bearings. We don't know exactly what route he took, but he ended up at the front door of the condo, where he unlocked the deadbolt, flipped the safety latches, opened the unwieldy door, and walked out to the fourteen-story atrium. Fortunately Paige had just dozed off, and when the sound of the closing door startled her awake, she hightailed it out of bed. She found her daddy a few doors down, near a bank of elevators, utterly confused about where he was.

Paige hugged his neck. And then she walked him home.

The next night, when Paige and I were putting the young'uns to bed, she mentioned her concern that Joe might unknowingly make a break for it again after everybody went to sleep. So before she turned in for the night, she moved four huge wrought-iron bar stools to block the path to the front door. She reasoned that even if Joe tried to move the bar stools, they'd scrape against the tile floor and someone would hear the racket.

My family was staying in the room across from Paige's family, and about one-thirty in the morning we heard a loud "SCRRREEEEEECH!" as Joe tried to slide one of the bar stools away from the door. Within seconds I heard Paige say, "Daddy! Hold on just a second, Daddy!" as she walked into the foyer. And for the second time in two nights, she led Joe back to where he was supposed to be.

It's a tricky thing, Alzheimer's—or any debilitating disease, for that matter. Caretakers and loved ones know they have to adjust to a new normal, but that new normal is a shifty rascal. One day Chox would feel like everything was under control because Joe had responded well to a new medication or because he seemed better adjusted to his schedule or because he was acclimating to new environments a little easier, only to realize several weeks or months later that Joe's condition was worse—again. Chox did everything she could to keep their lives as normal as possible, but caring for someone with a progressively debilitating disease is like trying to hold your balance on a high wire while juggling explosives. It's possible, of course, if you set your mind to it and devote your life to the task, but you certainly can't sustain the nonstop pace of the routine year after year after year. Because eventually, unless you're some sort of superhero, you'll fall down from sheer exhaustion, or something will blow up when you least expect it. And neither outcome is particularly desirable.

The weather forecast wasn't in our favor a couple of days later, and since Benji's girls wanted to do some back-to-school shopping (they were only ten and eight at the time, but they've always appreciated a cute outfit), we decided that an afternoon at the nearby outlet mall might be good for everybody. Since there were too many of us for one car, Alex hopped in Paige's SUV with all his cousins, and I jumped in the car with Chox and Joe. We had barely turned out of the condo entrance and onto the main road when we realized Joe had interpreted the fact that he was riding in a car as a sure sign that his wish was finally coming true.

"Choxie? We going to Prayer Meeting, Mama?"

"No, Joe," she replied. "I told you earlier. We're going to the outlet mall. The one at Foley."

"Foley?" Joe answered. "Not Myrtlewood? We're not going to Prayer Meeting?"

"No. We are not going to Prayer Meeting." Chox laughed. "We're going to the outlet mall."

Joe tried to put the pieces together for a second or two before he decided to be agreeable.

"Oh. Okay, then. If you say so."

Chox's eyes met mine in the rearview mirror. She just shook her head.

Joe was quiet from Orange Beach to the toll bridge, but as soon as the toll-bridge arm went up, it was like a lightbulb went on in his head. Maybe he remembered that they'd stopped to pay a toll on the way to the condo, or maybe the sight of the toll arm moving triggered a memory from years before. Regardless, Joe determined that Chox wasn't telling him everything, and he intended to get to the bottom of the situation.

"Choxie, are we going to Myrtlewood?"

"No, Joe. I told you. We're going to the outlet mall."

"Well, is that in Myrtlewood? Because I want to go to Prayer Meeting."

"Joe. We're not going to Myrtlewood. We're not going to Prayer Meeting. We're going to the outlet mall to look for some clothes for the girls."

"Will we be finished with that in time for Prayer Meeting?"

Chox's fingers tightened around the steering wheel as she dug deep for an extra measure of patience.

"Joe. We're at the beach. In Alabama. Myrtlewood is in Mississippi. We're not going to Mississippi. We're not going to Prayer Meeting. We are going to the outlet mall—the outlet mall that is here, at the beach, in Alabama. Got it?"

Joe shrugged and looked out the passenger window. His aggravation enveloped the car like a fog.

We'd been riding in silence for a mile or two when Chox noticed that her low-fuel light was on. Joe was presumably still steaming about Prayer Meeting and had been ignoring us, so it didn't even occur to Chox to mention the low-fuel light to him. She just offhandedly asked, "Hey, Soph—do you know if there are any gas stations around here?"

We assumed that Joe had tuned us out, but he snapped to attention like he was still in the Marines and was about to receive orders from a commanding officer. Really, Chox and I shouldn't have been surprised.

You see, even as he battled Alzheimer's, Joe maintained unwavering affection for a number of things in his life. God and country, certainly. Chox, Paige, Benji, and their families, absolutely. Next on his list was the business he and Chox had built together, followed closely by the Boy Scouts and the Ole Miss Rebels. And I believe his devotion to Prayer Meeting has been well documented.

But that list would be completely incomplete without mentioning the care with which Joe maintained his vehicles. Before

Alzheimer's had set in, he washed his and Chox's cars almost every weekend, and he always made sure everything was in order: plenty of air in the tires, plenty of oil, plenty of gas. He was the same way about his boats, and there were many weekends when he'd run up to their lake house just outside of town to inspect the boat covers, crank the motors, and double-check that everything was docked securely. After his doctors told him he shouldn't drive anymore, he couldn't handle the maintenance duties quite like he used to, but oh, he could keep an eye on a gas gauge. And for the most part, he did.

So when Chox mentioned the need for a gas station, Joe was on the case—Barney Fife in the flesh. He leaned waaaay over toward her side of the car, just as far as his seatbelt would allow, and said, "Hmph! You need some gas! You've got to get some gas! Why don't you have enough gas? Is Mr. Grant's place around here?"

Mr. Grant ran a full-service gas station in Myrtlewood from the '60s through the '90s. But we knew exactly what Joe meant.

Chox and I thought there were a couple of convenience stores a little closer to Foley, so we kept driving down the same highway, all the while listening as Joe wondered aloud why in the world Chox's car was almost out of gas. Every thirty seconds or so he'd lean over again to check the fuel gauge, and then he'd shake his head and grumble about whether we were going to make it to Mr. Grant's since Chox's tank was almost empty and the light was on and everything.

I believe with everything in me that, at that point, the Alzheimer's had almost nothing to do with Joe's reaction. Sick or no, Joe never would've let a fuel tank get below half full; that kind of reckless behavior was irresponsible, as far as he was concerned. So while he was fuzzy about Mr. Grant's role in the refueling process, he was totally true to character in his reaction. We might as well have been in Chox's wood-paneled Oldsmobile Custom Cruiser station wagon, traveling to Atlanta to see Sister's new apartment back in 1979. And if we *had* been in Chox's wood-paneled Oldsmobile Custom Cruiser station wagon back then, I probably would have been hanging out with Paige on the rear-facing vinyl seat, sporting some sweet Luv-It jeans with satin appliques and showing off the brand-new kelly green comb I liked to tuck in my back pocket. Chox would have been riding shotgun, turning around occasionally to snap her fingers at us, while Joe barreled down the interstate with one eye on the road and one eye on that fuel gauge. Just as the good Lord intended.

When Chox was driving that day in Foley, though, she grew increasingly weary of the constant fuel-gauge scrutiny from ole Eagle Eye over in the passenger seat. Finally—mercifully—we spotted a Texaco a little ways down the road, and when Chox pulled up to the pump and turned off the engine, she exhaled with all the force of a hurricane, it seemed. I jumped out of the car to fill 'er up while Chox dug through her purse for a credit card, and when at last she found her American Express and turned to hand it to me, Joe opened his door and bolted out of the car like a shot.

"Joe! Hold on, Joe! Where are you going?" Chox yelled.

"It's all right, Mama," he replied, waving her off. "I'm just gonna run inside and sign the ticket for Mr. Grant."

Chox started to stop him but thought better of it. No harm could come from Joe going inside a convenience store to sign a nonexistent ticket, so she let it go. A few seconds later Joe emerged from the store grinning like a kid with a pocketful of lollipops. He gave Chox a big thumbs-up.

After I finished filling up the car and settled back in my seat,

Chox exhaled one more time and cranked the car so we could head over to the outlet mall. She was just about to put the car in drive when Joe leaned over to check the gas gauge one more time.

"Well, it looks like you have plenty of gas!"

Then: "So. Are we going to Prayer Meeting, Mama?"

And that, my friends, was the proverbial straw that broke the Choxie's back. She leaned forward and rested her head on the steering wheel, and when she sat up again, I could see the frustration and sadness from the previous three or four days all over her face.

"Joe," she said in a calm, measured tone. "Look at me."

Their eyes met across the leather console that ran between their seats.

"We've covered this over and over again. We are not going to Prayer Meeting. We are NOT going to Prayer Meeting. Because, Joe? Where are we?"

Joe thought long and hard about her question. And after about fifteen seconds, he gave her his best, most honest answer.

"Heck if I know!" he exclaimed, and then he puckered up like a guppy, leaned over, and kissed her on the cheek.

There are certain times in life when you're not sure whether you should surrender to laughter or tears, and that was one of them. Within seconds, though, the bittersweet hilarity of the situation struck a collective nerve. All three of us guffawed until we hurt, and while tears were definitely simmering beneath the surface, that afternoon was a perfect reminder of the best parts of Chox and Joe's marriage. They had faced all sorts of difficulties together—including Alzheimer's—but I can't recall a single instance when they didn't trust each other completely, adore each other openly, and entertain each other to no end. And even though Joe's memory was failing him more and more by the day, it was obvious that his love for Chox wasn't anything he had to remember. It was a part of him that lived way down deep in his soul.

Anyone who has been married knows that the whole "for better or for worse, for richer or for poorer, in sickness and in health" thing is all fine and good and easy when you're twenty-four and wearing a pretty dress and fit as a fiddle and your hair is just like you like it and your direct deposit kicks in twice a month. But the character of a marriage is forged in the difficult times, when you're grappling with heartbreak or illness or disappointment or maybe even betrayal. So while, yes, the happy parts of Chox and Joe's marriage gave our family all sorts of wonderful memories, the way they loved each other in the hard parts? In the middle of an agonizing diagnosis?

You just can't underestimate the power of that example.

Later that night, after we'd recovered from our outlet mall adventure and nearly made ourselves sick on a supper of spicy boiled shrimp, green salad, and a feast o'carbs that we lovingly refer to as "beach taters," Chox and I were sitting at the table, running through the genealogy of Myrtlewood and cackling like crazy as we connected long-forgotten dots between families. About that time Joe opened the door to the balcony, looked outside, and said, "Come here. That, that . . ."—and he pointed to the sky in frustration as he searched for the word he needed, for the word that would not come.

So Chox and I walked outside, and we looked up at the sky, and Joe said, "Looka there. It's shining right down on that water."

Sure enough, there was the moon. In fact, it was the most stunning full moon I'd ever seen, hitting the Gulf like a spotlight. So we stood there, and we stared, and we sighed. It was beautiful. Joe couldn't take his eyes off of it. And finally, after several minutes, Chox broke the silence.

"It's the moon, Joe," she whispered, as she patted him gently on the shoulder.

Joe's eyes crinkled into a smile when he turned to look at his bride.

"Well, I'll be doggone," he said, with awe in his voice. "I'll be doggone."

CHAPTER TWELVE

Because Nothing Says "Welcome" like Rifling through a Handbag

ONE SUNDAY AFTERNOON Mama, Daddy, and Martha came to Birmingham so they could go to Grandparents' Day at Alex's school the next morning. Within five minutes of their arrival, I was driving Martha to Stein Mart, a totally unsurprising development considering that the only thing my mother-in-law loves more than going to Stein Mart is talking about what she'd like to find when she gets there. On that particular day the like-to-find was a pair of clip-on earrings with a purple stone in the center. Only not a real purply purple! More of a smoky purple! And it needed to be a round stone. A round stone!

So Martha and I went to Stein Mart. She found two jackets on the sale rack, and would you believe that one of the jackets was in a shade of green she does not own?

It's true!

The only possible reason for this phenomenon is that someone in a lab somewhere must have invented a new shade of green. There's just no other explanation.

Martha wanted to try on the jackets for me before she bought them, which basically means I held her purse and nodded while she pointed out the various features of the closures and the collars and the sleeves and the fit. After she'd covered the mechanics of the jackets, she moved on to creating a hypothetical list of all the places she'd be able to wear each one: "I think this one would be wonderful if I went out for a nice dinner or if we had a little Sunday school party or if I went somewhere fun with the girls! And I think this one—well, I could just throw this one on with my black pants or my taupe pants and it would be good anytime, really, because it's lined and casual but more of a coat! More of a light coat!"

And then my eyes rolled in opposite directions and I completely lost consciousness right there in the middle of the handbags.

After we left Stein Mart, we ran by a fast-food place so I could pick something up for supper because, well, I don't think there's anything quite like a family pack of spicy fried chicken to make guests feel right at home. While we were waiting at the window for our food, I asked Martha if she'd ever tried a milk shake from that restaurant. I explained that the milk shakes were absolutely delicious—the closest thing to homemade you can get at a fast-food place—and she said that she hadn't tried one but would absolutely love to because, after all, she was trying to gain some weight and I just had no idea, NO IDEA, how hard she'd been working to gain eight pounds! She really needed to gain eight pounds!

And she was right, of course. I don't have the foggiest idea what it's like to have to work at gaining weight. Because while I'm not good at much, gaining weight is something that I seem to be able to do fairly effortlessly. Perhaps I'm just gifted in that area. In fact, maybe I should volunteer to be Martha's weight-gaining mentor. I feel that I could be of some service.

Blessed to be a blessing!

After supper (and by the way, Martha agreed that the milk shake was delicious! just absolutely delicious! perfectly delicious!) we only visited for an hour or so before everybody agreed that they were ready for bed. It couldn't have been later than nine thirty when we all decided to turn in for the night, and let me tell you: I was borderline giddy at the thought of climbing into my bed and just *anticipating* sleep. The prospect of nine glorious hours of slumber filled my heart with joy. I was ready to SHUT 'ER DOWN and rest, oh, hallelujah.

Well.

About 2:40 on Monday morning, our dog woke me from a sleep so deep I wasn't entirely sure where I was when I opened my eyes. The dog needed to go outside, and it was no small feat that I managed to stumble out of our room without sustaining some sort of injury. I opened the front door, and as I watched the dog walk across the driveway, I noticed there was a light on inside Martha's car.

It was an unexpected middle-of-the-night complication, to say the least.

I walked over to the car in hopes that the doors were unlocked, but they weren't. That would have been way too easy. In my groggy state I tried to calculate how long the light must have been on—there were visions of dead car batteries dancing in my head—and I realized that it had to be at least six hours. I figured I'd better find Martha's keys sooner rather than later, but in all honesty, the part of me that was fully aware that it was 2:45 in the morning—and that I was about to execute a search for a set of keys—was not at all pleased.

I looked in the foyer, the kitchen, and the den, but there were no keys to be found. Then I remembered seeing Martha put her keys in her purse when we got home from Stein Mart, so I figured the purse was probably a critical component in the key quest. The problem, however, was that the purse was in the room where Martha was sleeping.

You can appreciate my dilemma.

With my phone in hand, I carefully opened the bedroom door, and then, using my phone as a flashlight, I tippy-toed over to Martha's purse. I grabbed it, backed out of the room, and hurried to the kitchen so I could pilfer through the contents of my mother-in-law's sensible black bag. I would try to explain just how awkward this whole scenario was except that *awkward* really isn't strong enough a word. There's no kind of premarital counseling that can prepare you for the day you'll be digging through a purse owned by your husband's mother and sifting through her stash of tissues and a small collection of mints.

I looked through every part of that purse at least three times, and after about five minutes I realized I was going to have to wake up Martha to ask where I could find her keys. At that point it was around three, so I knew that it was essential to keep the whole need-your-keys conversation as brief as possible so she'd still be able to go back to sleep once I left the room. It was a small key-finding window, if you will.

So. I took a deep breath, walked back to her bedroom, eased over to where she was sleeping, and said, "Martha?" very softly, hoping I wouldn't scare her out of her wits by standing over her bed at, you know, THREE IN THE MORNING.

At first she didn't answer, so I said, "Martha?" one more time, and oh my goodness, she sat up in that bed like a jack-in-the-box and said, "Is it time? Is it time to wake up? Time to get ready? I'm up! I'm up! I'm about to get ready!"

Using my very best Calm Voice, I tried to explain the

situation: "No, it's not time to get up. I just need your keys. There's a light on in your car, and I want to turn it off. But you don't need to get out of bed—just tell me where your keys are."

"My purse! My purse! They're in my purse! Will you hand me my purse? I think they're in my purse!"

So I handed her the purse, and she dug around and moved stuff and pulled out tissues and dug some more. In my best, most even-tempered whisper, I reminded her that she could just tell me where the keys were, that she didn't need to wake up all the way or get out of the bed, but she just kept on digging in that purse.

"They're in here! I just know they're in here! They're in one of these little compartments! There are just so many compartments!"

And then, I KID YOU NOT: "I'm just so happy to be here! I'm having a perfectly wonderful time!"

Well, sure she was. After all, what could be more fun than being awakened in the middle of the night by your daughter-in-law asking where she can find your keys? That's a fail-proof formula for some scrapbook-worthy moments, my friends.

Finally Martha realized that her keys were on top of her makeup bag, so I grabbed them, then quickly shut the bedroom door and walked back outside. Much to my relief, I finally turned off that blasted light. And since I was wide awake from the key hunt, I spent the rest of the night looking at people's pictures on Facebook and thinking about all the sleep I wasn't getting.

However, I found some small degree of comfort in knowing that middle-of-the-night car care might very well be one of my spiritual gifts.

Along with effortless weight gain, of course.

Sometimes you just have to take your victories wherever you can find them, I reckon.

CHAPTER THIRTEEN

Watching TV with My Daddy

Twenty-four-karat gold elegance manufactured especially for
click
And then the Blazers pushed down the floor with fifteen
click
EVERYBODY OUT OF HERE FAST! WE'RE NOT
GONNA MAKE IT IF
click
With just one spray of Plaque Attack, your dog's teeth
click
Coming up next on *The Real Housewives of Orange*
click
Sir, would you please tell us where you were on the night
of February
click
Speculation and scandal surrounding the CEO of
click

The barracuda has very large teeth and an underbite that
click
A local woman has discovered a way to create aprons from
click
What's not to like? Custard, GOOD. Jam, GOOD. Meat? GOOOOOD.
click
Standoff looking increasingly likely in negotiations with NATO
click
Whatcha up to, Opie?
Oh, don't mind me, Pa. I'm just about to go fishin'.
Barney? That you?
Yessir, Sheriff Taylor. Just wanted to stop by and tell you the latest with Otis.
clicking stops

And that's my daddy. No matter what's going on in the world, no matter what gimmicks or trends or trivia vie for his attention, he eventually makes his way back to Mayberry.

I didn't appreciate that as a little girl.

But as a grown-up?

I treasure it.

CHAPTER FOURTEEN

The Unexpected Ministry of the Cowbell

WHEN I WAS SEVEN years old, my parents took me to a basketball game at Mississippi State, my daddy's alma mater. The primary purpose of our trip was to watch Sister, who was a student at MSU, perform in a play at the student union, but Daddy also managed to get some tickets to that weekend's basketball game. I have no idea who we played, but I do remember that I had a killer earache and that Mama stuffed cotton in my left ear while we sat in our rafter-level seats at the brand-spankin' new Humphrey Coliseum.

Seriously. Between the cotton in my ear, my How to Roller-Skate T-shirt, and the fact that I probably imitated the Fonz and replied with "Ayyyyyy" to anyone who spoke to me before I stuck my nose back into whichever Boxcar Children book I was reading at the time, I think it's safe to say that I spent a significant portion of third grade standing at the intersection of Nerdy and Oblivious.

That weekend at State turned out to be like countless other short trips I took with my parents when I was younger—save one critical detail. Because at some point while I sat at that basketball game, cotton eared and all, I decided that I was a Bulldog. Until then I'd vacillated between cheering for State and cheering for Ole Miss, the Bulldogs' in-state archrival about a hundred miles up the road. Many of my relatives were (and are) dyed-in-the-wool Rebels—I even have a cousin who was a starter on the football team in the early '70s—and my brother was planning to enroll at Ole Miss the following fall. I'd listened to Joe wax poetic about Archie Manning all my life, and I'd heard my cousins yell Ole Miss's "Hotty Toddy" cheer (with some creative substitutions for four-letter words) for as long as I could remember.

Considering the family dynamics, it probably would have been easier to be an Ole Miss fan and join the vocal majority of my kinfolk. But loyalty to my daddy and my sister won out; I decided at that basketball game that I was going to err on the side of maroon.

It's a little astonishing to me that I have any recollection of making a choice, but Sister says it shouldn't surprise me at all. Her theory is that growing up in Mississippi and eventually picking a team to root for is sort of like being baptized: you never forget the moment it happens, and there's no turning back after you take the plunge.

The complex dynamics in the State–Ole Miss rivalry eluded me when I was a little girl; I just thought that the red-and-blue team waved flags during their games and the maroon-and-white team rang cowbells. Now, however, I know that if you dig way down to the core of why the battle between the two teams often gets so heated, you'll find some good, old-fashioned conflict between the classes.

Many State folks pride themselves on being hardworking, salt-of-the-earth people who don't mind getting their hands dirty in the interest of the greater good. Ole Miss, on the other hand, produces most of Mississippi's doctors and lawyers, and as a result, they have a reputation for being cultured, well-to-do, and according to some of their alumni, better educated than their Bulldog brethren to the south. In fact, a few years ago, when MSU football coach Dan Mullen began a little good-natured gamesmanship by referring to Ole Miss as "the school up north"—TSUN for short—some Ole Miss faithful fired back by referring to State as "the school beneath us."

So there you have it. Make of it what you will.

For the longest time I thought the rivalry developed once the two teams started playing football against each other in 1901, but it actually started much earlier than that. According to *Sports Illustrated* writer Ed Hinton, the battle between the two schools began in 1872, when the Mississippi legislature tried to attach an agriculture school to Ole Miss. They found a dean, planned a curriculum, and after all the arrangements were made, an unexpected problem arose: nobody showed up for class. Hinton quotes Dr. David Sansing, then a professor of history at Ole Miss, as saying that "the sons of the industrial classes didn't want to go up to Ole Miss, where they would have to go to school with the sons of the gentry."

Just for the record, Sister and I have often speculated that at least a couple of those students who refused to go to school in Oxford are bound to have been some of our daddy's ancestors. He comes from a mighty long line of stubborn, principled men.

Anyway, Hinton goes on to say that since no one wanted to attend an agriculture school in Oxford, "an entirely new school was created in Starkville . . . [and] quickly acquired a popular nickname: People's College. No vestiges of class structure, such as those that prevailed at Ole Miss, were allowed at what would become Mississippi State."

By the way, sometimes when I need to smile, I like to find Hinton's article on the Internet and reread that last sentence. It sums up everything I love about Mississippi State. And just to be clear: Ole Miss is a great school. Oxford is a wonderful place. Some of my closest friends are Rebels. State just happens to be where I belong. And somehow I knew that when I was seven years old.

Once my allegiance to the 'Dogs was settled, Daddy wasted no time capitalizing on my interest in All Things Maroon and White. We went to alumni association meetings in Myrtlewood, tuned in to a local AM station to listen to Jack Cristil's play-by-play of football and basketball games, and started a tradition of going to all of the home football games together when I was in seventh grade. Now that I'm a grown-up, it's not lost on me that Daddy always made time to take me. His job at the Cooperative Extension Service was a demanding one, and he also officiated high school football games every Friday night during football season, but as sure as the sun, he'd wake up early on Saturday mornings and drive us to Starkville. Our season tickets were his promise to spend time with me, and he never broke his word.

Mama would usually pack us a lunch of fried chicken, potato salad, and sweet tea, and once we arrived on State's campus, we'd meet up with some of Daddy's Extension Service buddies for a tailgate lunch. Everybody shared whatever they'd brought—hot dogs, burgers, chips, dips, brownies—and after the ladies finished setting up a makeshift buffet table, it always looked like we were rehearsing for Thanksgiving dinner. I loved to sit and soak up the adults' stories about their days at State, and they never made it more than about three sentences before someone would mention the name of an MSU great: Shorty McWilliams, Rockey Felker, Bailey Howell, Johnie Cooks, and so many more. Tailgating was always a history lesson.

Daddy and I usually walked into the stadium just as warm-ups started—a habit that has stayed with me through three decades and countless games. We probably saw the Bulldogs lose more than we saw them win, but their end-of-season record wasn't really the point. Those days at Scott Field were much more about family and loyalty and fellowship. Winning was just gravy, really.

With one exception.

Once a year—usually on the Saturday after Thanksgiving—the Bulldogs and the Rebels would play the annual Egg Bowl in Jackson. And winning that game? Oh, it mattered. Losing meant I'd have to listen to my brother and my cousins assert their gridiron superiority for what seemed like a sweet forever. Losing meant Joe would print Christmas cards of the scoreboard, and I'd have to smile and laugh it off and pretend like I didn't care. Losing meant I'd have to humble myself in front of my friend Jon at school on Monday morning. One year, in fact, when State lost after a gust of wind suddenly stopped a potentially game-winning field goal in midair and slammed it to the ground, Jon and his daddy actually made a huge sign and staked it across our front yard.

Jon's daddy was a Southern Baptist preacher and a lifelong Rebel fan. Apparently, in the Lord's eyes, those two things aren't mutually exclusive.

(I smiled when I typed that, by the way.)

(I promise.)

So *winning* the Egg Bowl? That was an infinitely preferable option. Winning meant Daddy and I could walk back to our car after the game without listening to some overserved Ole Miss students scream, "COW COLLEGE!" at any State fans who happened to pass by. Winning meant the Sunday edition of the *Clarion-Ledger* would be chock-full of Mississippi State goodness that I could pin to my bulletin board. Winning meant I could wear my snazzy MSU V-neck sweater to church. Winning meant bragging rights for the next year, and I knew from experience that those bragging rights had a way of making life just a little bit easier.

I don't think Daddy and I missed a single Egg Bowl between my junior high days and my senior year in high school. A few years later, when I was a junior at State, I made what would be my final Egg Bowl pilgrimage to Jackson. The game was being moved back to the schools' campuses the next year, and I wanted to be there for the last Veterans Stadium hurrah. There was a horrible, bench-clearing brawl before the game even started, and after four quarters of agonizingly slow football, the Rebels were victorious. I would tell you that it was a super-fun day, but that would be a lie. It was miserable.

🌹

Over the next few years my Egg Bowl attendance was spotty at best; I didn't trust myself to maintain a proper perspective if I went to the game in Oxford (especially if, heaven forbid, we lost), and after I got married and moved to Louisiana, it wasn't exactly convenient to make the five-hour journey to Starkville.

Once we were in Birmingham, it seemed like it would be easier than ever to get back in the swing of going to the games. But then I got pregnant. And then I had a baby who eventually became a toddler. And despite the fact that I'd always seen mamas with young kids at the games and thought it would be

super easy to juggle caring for a youngster with watching the
revelry on the field, it turned out I was dead wrong. The good
Lord did not gift me with that particular skill set.

Once Alex hit six years old, however, traveling with him to
games became absolutely delightful. And after an especially fun
trip to watch State play Florida in 2009, we decided that the
little man was ready for his very first Egg Bowl. I didn't know
how he would handle the State vs. Ole Miss scenario since he
has always felt a certain degree of cousin-prompted loyalty to the
Rebels, but I figured we'd give it a go and see what happened.

The day before the game we drove to Memphis to celebrate
my brother's birthday. My sister-in-law Janie was surprising him
with a party that Friday night, and since Sister and Barry were
going to be in Memphis, too, we figured it was a perfect opportunity for the MSU branch of the family tree to wake up at the
crack of light on Saturday morning, stop by Starbucks, and then
caravan to Starkville for the game.

Sister and I love to go to games together whenever we can,
and we have made some mighty fine memories over the years.
Once, in the days before I realized that wrangling a toddler at
a sporting event was not necessarily my forte, Sister and I traveled to Tuscaloosa—with eleven-month-old Alex in tow—and
watched State's men's basketball team play Alabama for the SEC
regular season title. Bulldog fans packed out the upper deck, so
the atmosphere was festive, to say the least. Sister and Alex even
ran into Bulldog coaching legend Jackie Sherrill when they were
making a few loops around the concourse right after halftime,
and in my opinion it was a sign that the Lord had granted the
Bulldogs an extra measure of favor. Sure enough, the 'Dogs won
in overtime, and Sister gave Alex a celebratory bottle while his
mama (that would be me) jumped up and down in the aisle of

Coleman Coliseum like some sort of hillbilly game-show contestant. It was a fantastic day.

Five and a half years later, we were hoping to make some maroon-colored memories with Alex all over again.

By six o'clock that Saturday morning, we were pulling onto Highway 78 outside Memphis so we could make the 11:30 kickoff in Starkville. Sister and Barry were in one car; David, Alex, and I were in another. From Olive Branch to Tupelo, cars zoomed past with various forms of Rebel and Bulldog paraphernalia flapping in the chilly November air, and once we turned onto Highway 45 in Tupelo, we joined a slower game-day processional that moved through some of my favorite Mississippi towns: Verona, Okolona, West Point. Traffic was slow, but it was moving, and even though there were no girls sitting on the backs of convertibles waving to the crowd, it might as well have been a parade. Every once in a while we'd hear somebody ringing a cowbell or screaming, "Go Rebels" while we waited at a red light, and I wondered how many times a variation of that scene had played out over the years.

I'm pretty sure it was more than twice.

We stopped outside West Point so we could fill up our respective cars, and within seconds of our arrival, a Hummer limousine pulled in behind us. Ole Miss flags flanked the back windows, and the passengers crawled out holding monogrammed Tervis tumblers (full to the brim with the passengers' beverages of choice) and sporting the latest Tory Burch tunics. As they dug through their Louis Vuitton cross-body bags for their lip gloss, Sister and I started to laugh. We were both nursing the last of our Venti Pike Place coffees from Starbucks, wearing our finest Old Navy duds, and singing the praises of some crazy-comfortable fleece-lined clogs to which we are both completely addicted—not to mention that we were both carrying large metal cowbells with welded handles in our sensible Stein Mart purses. We were an unintended study in State and Ole Miss contrasts, and after the fellas finished filling up the cars, I took one more look at that Hummer limo before I grinned at Sister and said two of our very favorite words: "Go 'Dogs."

"Go 'Dogs," she replied.

Forty-five minutes later we pulled into our parking places on State's campus, and even though it wasn't quite nine o'clock in the morning, the atmosphere was electric. The next hour and a half flew by; we greeted the players at Dawg Walk, welcomed the Rebels to the stadium with some (mostly) good-natured cowbell ringing, strolled through the bookstore, visited with my friend Daphne and her family, and sampled a few of Daph's mini quiches and fried catfish filets. I don't want to overstate the impact of a fried catfish filet on a football game, but my personal experience has been that if some fried catfish can't get your game-day motor running, you might be due for some service.

That's all I'm saying.

Around ten fifteen we settled into our seats in the stadium, at which point Sister and I noticed an especially vocal Rebel fan to our left. We both had flashbacks to a couple of years before, when an elderly woman who was cheering for the Rebels sat about four rows below us. When Ole Miss scored a first quarter touchdown, the woman stood up, turned around, cupped her hands around her mouth, and screamed, "HOTTY TODDY!" at the section where we were sitting. I've been in situations where State fans fired back at an outspoken Rebel or maybe even responded with a little hostility, but on that day the State folks didn't say a word. However, when State scored two touchdowns

125

in the fourth quarter and tied the game, the indignant Rebel threw her hands up in the air, gave the Ole Miss coach a piece of her mind, and then slammed her stadium seat shut. She glared at our section, gathered her belongings, and marched up the stairs to a chorus of spontaneous applause from the four hundred or so State fans who had witnessed her performance in the first quarter and were none too sad to see her pack her toys and go home.

I don't judge that woman for one second, by the way. I'm all too aware that, during football season, I'm pretty much one play away from a total nervous breakdown at any given point in time. And if you think I'm kidding, just ask my daddy, who had to sit with me at Long John Silver's in Starkville and talk me off the emotional ledge after a particularly nasty loss to Auburn in the mid '80s.

Sister and I need not have worried at the 2009 Egg Bowl, though, because the pretty Rebel fan to our left was a nonfactor. She yelled for her team, which was certainly to be expected, but when the Bulldogs scored seventeen points in the third quarter and jumped out to a fourteen-point lead, our Rebel neighbor gave up cheering and comforted herself by talking on her phone, then resorting to some rapid-fire texting for the remainder of the game. It's a shame the Rebels didn't have her thumbs playing on offense—they were blazing fast and probably could have run about a 4.3 forty-yard dash.

The girl acted oblivious to a positively raucous Scott Field, which was the loudest I've ever heard it. Eventually the noise hit a level that couldn't possibly increase, so people took their cheering to the next level and started to jump. It didn't matter how old they were, how young they were, or how fit they were—everyone jumped. And by the beginning of the fourth quarter, the stadium wasn't so much a building as it was a living, moving, cowbell-ringing *creature*. The sound was like a thousand thunderstorms pounding on a thousand tin roofs—all set to the rhythm of techno music blaring through giant speakers. It couldn't have been fun for the loyal Rebels who were still scattered throughout the stands. But for the Bulldogs?

Oh, make no mistake.

It was glorious.

The smile on our little guy's face was as wide as the Mississippi River as he soaked in the craziness and the chaos of Davis Wade Stadium, and one look at him let me know the die was cast. He was a Bulldog too. It was oddly sweet to know that the matter of his college loyalty was settled—at least for the time being. Mock me if you must, but there's a definite "awwww" factor to knowing your child has decided that he's a part of your team, so to speak.

Once the game was over, Sister, Alex, and I stayed behind to savor the postgame atmosphere while David and Barry made a beeline for Daph's tailgating tent. The three of us stood in front of our seats and watched players circle the field, holding the Egg Bowl trophy high above their heads while the fight song ricocheted off the field house and wrapped the bleachers in the sounds of "Hail State." Eventually we joined the crowd of folks who were slowly walking down the south ramp of the stadium. Alex hopped and jumped more than he walked, and every once in a while Sister or I would have to remind him to stay with us and not get too far ahead. The maroon hood of his Mississippi State sweatshirt twisted and danced all the way down the ramp; there wasn't a doubt in my mind that he'd caught the fever.

And the only prescription?

MORE COWBELL.

I've heard my pastor say more than once that, if we don't keep it in check, college football can be an idol—especially in the South, where national championships abound and people can quote a prospective quarterback's passing percentage easier than they can quote a passage of Scripture.

I know exactly what he means. I have a personality that tends to err on the side of obsessive, and if I'm not careful, I can get caught up in the hype of a new season, in the off-the-field message-board drama, in the prospect of championships and trophies and recruiting dominance. And that's why the 2009 Egg Bowl—a day when the Bulldogs won 41–27, a day that turned out to be one of my favorite memories *ever*—is a perfect picture of what I want for our boy *and* what I don't want for him. All at the same time.

Confused yet?

Stay with me.

I will absolutely love it if Alex grows up and wants to go to college at State. I will be thrilled to pieces if he is the third generation of our family to earn a degree there. I will be beside myself if, ten years from now, David and I spend five or six fall weekends a year in Starkville, hanging out with our son and cheering for the Bulldogs and serving plates of pregame fried catfish to him and to his buddies. It would tickle me to no end.

But.

I want so much more for Alex Hudson than thinking the end-all, be-all of life is to sit in a stadium and watch twenty-two guys battle it out on a field. I want so much more for him than viewing the numbers on a scoreboard as a gauge for happiness. I want so much more for him than basing the sum total of his identity on an institution, a sports team, a career, or a player.

Because what I want for him more than anything else is for him to follow Jesus with every bit of the fervor, passion, and excitement we saw that day in Starkville. If he is going to completely abandon himself to any purpose, any cause, any greater good, please, Lord, *let it be Jesus.*

Please.

From the time Alex was a baby, I've prayed Ephesians 3:16-19 for him: "that according to the riches of his glory he may grant you to be strengthened with power through his Spirit in your inner being, so that Christ may dwell in your hearts through faith—that you, being rooted and grounded in love, may have strength to comprehend with all the saints what is the breadth and length and height and depth, and to know the love of Christ that surpasses knowledge, that you may be filled with all the fullness of God."

As a mama, it's good for me to remember that passage. I mean, I'm crazy about football, but I have sense enough to know that Paul wasn't writing to the church at Ephesus about the roots that run underneath the turf at Scott Field, you know?

Undoubtedly there's a time and a place for game-day enthusiasm. There's a time and a place for team loyalty, for family tradition, for ringing a cowbell, and for jumping up and down in a stadium.

But I pray that those things are never the objects of our little guy's worship.

I guess it's not too far outside the realm of possibility that by the time Alex is an adult, there will be some church somewhere that incorporates cowbells, Jumbotrons, and "Sandstorm" into their music ministry (though I pray my sweet mama isn't alive to see it; she still hasn't gotten over the fact that we're members of a church here in Birmingham where drums and instruments that require electricity are a regular part of our worship services). Even so, I hope Alex knows that a Saturday at Davis Wade Stadium will always pale in comparison to knowing, loving, and serving the living God. I hope he knows that there's no greater adventure than following wherever the Lord leads.

And I just wanted to go on the Official Spiritual Legacy Record and make that perfectly clear. Because as a friend of mine said one time, "Football is a great game, but it's an awful god."

However, I think it's worth noting that if the Bulldogs can beat the Rebels every November until Jesus returns—well, there's not a doubt in my mind that it will make eternity all the sweeter.

Especially since I'm fully convinced that there will be some cowbells mixed in with all those harps and lyres and trumpets in heaven.

And I'm pretty sure that Sister and Daddy would agree.

Go 'Dogs.

CHAPTER FIFTEEN

Saturday Lunch and the Fine Art of Funeral Planning

It's no secret that Southerners love their grandmothers. People in other parts of the country love their grandmothers too, of course, but in the South we tend to put them on a bit of a pedestal. We even give them funny names: MiMi, Grand, Shug, MawMaw, Honey, Nana, GiGi—and that's just the tip of the MeMaw iceberg. Since I called both of my grandmothers "Mamaw," I was in the Southern grandmother nickname mainstream, but David—well, he hit the jackpot. He grew up with two grandmothers who were affectionately called Mammy and Sissie.

Those are some good'uns, y'all.

Mammy died when David was a little boy, but Sissie was an ever-present matriarch throughout his childhood, high school days, college years, and adult life. She didn't rule with an iron fist by any stretch of the imagination; she preferred to make the occasional pointed suggestion with a can of Aqua Net in one hand and a glass of sweet tea in the other. If she was playing bridge with her friends, she'd trade that glass of sweet tea for a glass of Pink Catawba wine, but only in moderation, of course. Sissie was far too sensible to dabble in excess.

Unlike many women of her generation, Sissie worked outside the home. She and her husband, Bill, owned a floor-covering business, and when Bill died unexpectedly of a heart attack at forty-nine, Sissie became one of the few full-time businesswomen in 1950s-era Myrtlewood. Martha has told me many times that there wasn't a single aspect of the floor-covering industry that Sissie—who was "smart as a whip! just as smart as a whip!"— didn't know backward and forward, and her hard work kept Cooley Tile going. Sissie eventually sold the business, but she worked until she was in her early seventies, drove a car until she was in her eighties, and swept her driveway until she was well into her nineties.

A couple of years ago David, Alex, and I made a day trip to Myrtlewood, mainly so we could visit Sissie. Even though she was 101 at the time, she'd been in a local nursing home for only about five years. Before that she lived in the house she and Bill had built on a wide boulevard in the center of town. Until she fell and broke her hip one day when she tried to sit down in her recliner and misjudged the distance, one of her very favorite activities was raking the yard. David and I actually gave her a really good rake when she turned ninety-three— NINETY-THREE—and she was so thrilled by it you'd have thought we'd given her buckets of diamonds and gold.

Only, truth be told, Sissie wouldn't have enjoyed buckets of diamonds and gold nearly as much as she enjoyed that rake. She was practical to a fault.

Sissie adjusted remarkably well to life in the nursing home, in large part because Martha visited her at least twice a day. Honestly, I'm not sure which one of them depended on the other more: Sissie loved Martha's company, and Martha loved taking care of Sissie. Since Martha's husband, Dan, died after a long battle with cancer when Martha was still in her fifties, she and Sissie had been inseparable for the better part of twenty years. And when Sissie moved to the nursing home, there wasn't a single aspect of Sissie's new living situation that Martha didn't supervise, from medication to laundry to meals. Martha even made sure the hairstylists and nurses' aides were aware of Sissie's high expectations for her personal appearance. Martha reminded them time and time again that Sissie liked her hair to look pretty, and when they seemed to have trouble remembering the finer points of Sissie's hairdo, Martha left a note for them on Sissie's closet door:

> *Please help her keep her hair in place and lift her hair a little bit so it will stay set until Thursdays. It will not stay set if it gets wet.*
>
>

Many, many thanks,
Martha

> *P.S. Thanks for all you do for my mother.*

Martha actually gave a strong hair-care word when she pointed out that "it will not stay set if it gets wet." That's precisely why legions of mamas stick only their legs in the pool when they take their kids swimming. Furthermore, I believe that Martha has provided the perfect way for me to answer the next time my fellas want me to go on one of those theme park rides where you have to ride a faux-wood boat through a man-made monsoon: "IT WILL NOT STAY SET IF IT GETS WET." That's a hard hair truth.

I may need to pause for a minute and give the Lord a hand clap of praise.

Anyway, when the first note didn't do the trick, Martha's frustration grew, so she added a second, more direct note to the closet door:

> *Please don't brush Mother's bangs straight back anymore.*
> *Thanks,*
> *Martha*

Oh, Martha meant business about those bangs. And that last note, by the way, is as close to a Martha Smackdown as you can get. But really, if you think about it, we should all be as fortunate as Sissie to have someone who consistently advocates for our medical needs as well as the proper styling and care of our bangs. Martha took Sissie's hair standards seriously, and she stood firm when those standards weren't met. I'm pretty sure that's biblical.

During her time in the nursing home, Sissie remained sharp as a tack mentally, but physically she had a tougher time. And when David, Alex, and I set off on our day trip (Remember when I mentioned that? About sixty-five paragraphs ago?), we knew she had been dealing with some new-to-her issues. She was sleeping more and having some respiratory trouble, but even so, we were hopeful she'd be better soon. My mama, however, anticipated that our visit to the nursing home might be more difficult than we thought, so she asked us—and Martha—to come by her house for lunch before we went to see Sissie. My parents and Martha have been in the same Sunday school class since I was in third grade, so Martha has been like family since long before David and I got married. Plus, Mama's spiritual gifts are hospitality and mercy, and those gifts? Well, they like to make everybody feel better.

We arrived at Mama and Daddy's about the same time Martha

did, and Mama had prepared one of my favorite lunches: turkey divan, butter beans, strawberry congealed salad, rolls, and ice cream pie. Mama had decorated her dining room table by tucking hot-pink blooms into vases and underneath table runners and around an impressive array of candlesticks. I laughed to myself, because if I tried to replicate the same look in my own dining room, it would look like an azalea bush exploded into a hundred scattered pieces. But on Mama's table? It was a stunning symphony of spring.

After the usual pleasantries, our lunch conversation turned to a wedding that a friend of Mama's had directed a few months prior. In most Southern churches there is a female church member who handles the wedding-directing duties for the congregation, and her service is more valuable than many people realize. For one thing, this woman steps in to offer wise counsel if, say, an overzealous bride wants to bedeck the baptismal font with iridescent tulle and four feet of twinkle lights. She also makes sure the wedding music is appropriate for a house of worship, because while "Can You Feel the Love Tonight?" might have moved a bride to tears when she was in fifth grade and pictured herself singing it to her Prince Charming on her wedding day, that doesn't necessarily mean it's the best fit for a seven o'clock wedding in a conservative Presbyterian church. I once even heard about a Methodist wedding where, in a shocking breach of church policy, a bride and groom incorporated a boom box and an instrumental track of Clint Black and Lisa Hartman-Black's late '90s hit, "When I Said I Do," into their ceremony. They opted to sing it to each other after lighting the unity candle, and while it's very touching that they felt that way about one another, a good wedding director will tell brides (and grooms) that getting through the wedding ceremony without picking up a microphone to sing a country duet is a fine and noble goal indeed.

A wedding director also plans where the various members of the wedding party will stand during the ceremony, so her presence at the wedding rehearsal is critical. I've been in weddings where the director ran a rehearsal like a military exercise, to the point that the other bridesmaids and I muttered various iterations of "She scares me" under our breath while we practiced holding our bouquets just as the wedding director instructed: tulip blooms to the left, stems at a slight angle, right hand cradling the base of the bouquet, DO YOU UNDERSTAND?

For the most part, though, wedding directors tend to be gracious, warm, and charming, and since they're such an integral part of the wedding rehearsal and the wedding day, they're typically invited to the bride and groom's rehearsal dinner. Mama's friend—we'll call her Glenda—knows all about the rehearsal-dinner routine. She has directed hundreds of weddings over the last twentyish years, and as a result, Glenda has spent many a Friday night in a local restaurant/country club/family member's home while she enjoyed Some Form of Chicken Breast along with tearful toasts and general pre-wedding merriment. But for one particular wedding Glenda directed the previous February, an invitation to the rehearsal dinner never arrived. It was an unprecedented development in Glenda's stint as the church wedding director. And when Mama relayed this bit of news to Martha, a look of utter horror crossed Martha's face.

"Ouida!" Martha exclaimed. "You don't mean!"

"I *do* mean!" Mama replied. "They didn't send her an invitation. Never even mentioned it!"

"Ouida! I've just never in my whole life! I've never! After all the work it takes to direct a wedding? And they just didn't invite her? I've never!"

By then David, Daddy, and I were eyeballing each other,

knowing full well that it was pointless to try to inject any perspective into the tale of wedding-director woe. After a few minutes, though, I couldn't resist, so I said, "You know, I think I'd be relieved if I were Glenda. I'd much rather be at home than spend two hours at a formal rehearsal dinner."

Mama and Martha didn't say a word, but they stared at me like I had horns covered with white satin and seed pearls growing out of my head. Mama was no doubt feeling like she had failed at teaching me the finer points of Southern wedding etiquette, so I decided the safest course of action was to change the subject.

"Martha, how's Sissie doing? Is she starting to bounce back?" I asked, all the while silently double-dog-daring David and Daddy to bring up the name *Glenda* again.

"You know," Martha answered, "I think she's doing okay. She's definitely not as strong as she was the last time you saw her, but she's hanging in there. She's remarkable, Mother is. She really is remarkable!"

Martha's tone was cheerful enough, but I've known her since I was seven years old. I spent countless hours at her house when David and I were buddies in college. I've been her daughter-in-law for more than fifteen years. Seeing her twist her napkin and look down at her plate while she talked about Sissie told me everything she *wasn't* saying. Regardless of how she sounded, she was worried. And on some level, I think, she was scared.

❧

After we finished our turkey divan and put the hurt on the ice cream pie, David, Alex, and I rolled away from the table and got ready to head to the nursing home. Martha wanted us to run by her house first, so we said good-bye to Mama and Daddy and drove the four whole blocks between their place and Martha's.

We'd been inside for just a few seconds when Martha called me to her guest bedroom.

"Sophie, I know you probably don't want to think about this, because, well, *I* certainly don't want to think about this, but if Mother, you know—if she, *you know*—well, I was wondering if you think this pink suit or this blue suit would be prettier."

I had no idea what she was talking about. If Sissie *what?* I wondered. *If she went to church? If she entered one of those nursing-home beauty pageants? If she needed to interview for a job? Why in the world would Sissie need a suit?* Martha's question confounded me, so I looked at the two suits, then at Martha, then back at the suits, trying with everything in me to figure out what was going on. Apparently the expression on my face conveyed my confusion, so Martha tried to explain.

"Mother isn't—well, she isn't doing very well. Oh, she still knows me! She knows me! And she's still so dear! But she's taken a turn over the last few days, and I don't think"—she paused to clear her throat—"I don't think it'll be that much longer."

Suddenly I understood why we were looking at suits.

"I didn't want to upset y'all," Martha continued, "so I didn't say anything on the phone. But I think this blue suit is pretty, don't you? And blue is such a pretty color on Mother! Such a pretty color! This pink is pretty, too, though—but I worry that it'll be a little too low cut, and Mother wouldn't care for that, you know."

She was right. Sissie would have been mortified if anyone thought she was being laid to her eternal rest in anything even remotely resembling a plunging V-neck.

After considering the pros and cons of each suit while we stood in the guest room closet, Martha and I concluded that if someone could cut a panel for the front of the jacket, the pink suit would definitely be the better choice. We managed to have the entire conversation without using the words *death*, *dying*, *dead*, or *funeral*—a feat of discretion (with some denial mixed in for good measure) that shocks me even now. And with the suit issue settled, it was time to go to the nursing home.

Usually when we visited Sissie we'd find her in a wheelchair in the hallway outside her room. That's where the nursing-home residents liked to sit and visit. My sister-in-law Rose and I always marveled that Sissie sometimes struggled to hear the two of us, even if we screamed, but if Alex or his cousin Melissa whispered from forty feet away, Sissie immediately greeted them with "Oh, honey, come here! I sure am glad to see you!"

This phenomenon played out over and over again. In fact, when we'd gone to see Sissie the previous Christmas, she acted like she couldn't hear a word we said for the first thirty minutes of our visit. Martha was insistent that the hearing aid device in one of Sissie's dresser drawers might help, but then she realized that the battery in the hearing aid thingy was dead, so she took matters into her own hands by putting her face approximately a quarter inch away from Sissie's ear and saying, "Mother? Can you hear? Can you hear, Mother? Sugar, can you hear? Can you hear us, darlin'?"

And after about the eighth time Martha asked, Sissie whipped her head around and said, "I CAN HEAR, MARTHA! I CAN HEAR!"

So the issue wasn't that Sissie *couldn't* hear as much as it was that sometimes she just *chose* not to. And that was fine. At 101 years old, she'd earned the selective-hearing privilege.

But after we arrived at the nursing home that May afternoon, Sissie's hearing was the least of our worries. It was immediately evident that she was having a hard time. She was lying in her bed—not sitting in her wheelchair—and her breathing was labored and shallow. Martha remarked that her condition was worse than it had been the day before, and as Alex and I sat in the chair beside Sissie's bed and watched Martha rub Sissie's hands and gently ask how she was feeling, the realization that Sissie wasn't long for the world started to settle in. In the strangest, most unexpected way, I was shocked that it might be the last time we'd see Sissie alive. You'd think that death would pretty much be a foregone conclusion when you're talking about a 101-year-old, but Sissie had been a force in the Hudson family for so long that we'd halfway started to believe she'd outlive all of us.

That Sunday at the nursing home, however, was a fresh reminder that the Lord has numbered all of our days. Even Sissie's. Martha looked across Sissie's bed and said she didn't know what she'd do without her sweet mother, that it had been her great joy to take care of Sissie. That being said, she would never, ever want her mother to suffer, and she was grateful for the privilege of having had so many years with her.

After we talked to Scott and Rose and made sure Martha was okay, we drove back to Birmingham late Sunday afternoon. Three days later Martha called to tell us that Sissie had passed away. She'd lived a good, sweet, long life, and when she left it, she was bound to nothing except the extravagant grace of God.

Thursday morning we drove back to Myrtlewood, and the day was a blur of phone calls, funeral arrangements, and visits from Martha's friends. I happened to be at Martha's house when her neighbors Gertrude and Doris stopped by. Apparently, in the midst of making all the arrangements, Martha had completely forgotten to let them know about Sissie. When they found out from another neighbor, they immediately walked over to check on their dear friend.

As soon as Martha opened her door, Gertrude and Doris

hugged her neck and spent the next three or four minutes alternating questions.

"Martha, are you okay, darlin'?"

"Martha, why didn't you tell us?"

"Martha, is there anything we can do?"

"Martha, do you know when visitation will be?"

"Martha, why didn't you tell us?"

"Martha, have you talked to the preacher?"

"Martha, have you picked out the music?"

"Martha, why didn't you tell us?"

I came to a couple of conclusions as I listened to their questions. One was that they loved Martha to the moon and back.
The other was that when it comes to matters of death, the over-
sixty-five set likes to be informed as quickly as possible. Martha
did her best to convey the craziness of the previous twenty-four
hours, and she said, "I meant to let you know! I really did! But
you just can't even imagine how nonstop things have been! You
just can't even imagine! The phone has been ringing nonstop,
and I've been on my land phone and my cordless phone and my
cell phone all at the same time! My land phone and my cordless
phone and my cell phone! All at the same time!"

I don't think Martha ever realized that her land phone and her
cordless phone are the same thing, and honestly, that pesky little
detail was hardly worth clarifying. The point was that Martha was
overwhelmed, and after she told Gertrude and Doris about the
land phone and the cordless phone and the cell phone, she sank
into one of her dining room chairs and rested her head in her
hands. Gertrude and Doris immediately moved to either side of
Martha's chair and patted her back while they consoled her. The
tenderness of the moment struck me as I stood in Martha's kitchen
and scooped tablespoons of Maxwell House into the coffeepot.

The attentiveness these women showed to Martha was the picture of 2 Corinthians 1:3-5: "Praise be to the God and Father of our Lord Jesus Christ, the Father of compassion and the God of all comfort, who comforts us in all our troubles, so that we can comfort those in any trouble with the comfort we ourselves receive from God. For just as we share abundantly in the sufferings of Christ, so also our comfort abounds through Christ" (NIV).

In true Martha fashion, she allowed herself approximately one minute of sadness before she asked Gertrude and Doris if they'd like to stay for a little longer and maybe have some cake and coffee.

That's the thing about steel magnolias. They never wilt. And they're fueled by sugar and caffeine.

In keeping with Sissie's no-nonsense approach to, well, *everything*, Martha planned a simple, sweet funeral. After selecting the pink suit for Sissie (complete with a custom-made panel for the jacket), Martha decided to have visitation for an hour on Friday morning, followed by a graveside service at a nearby cemetery. The visitation—which was held at the church where Sissie had worshiped and served faithfully for more than sixty years, the church where Mama, Daddy, and Martha are still active members—the church where David and I grew up and got married— was an incredibly touching testimony to the impact of Sissie's life. The line of people who came to pay their respects stretched down the center aisle, through the foyer, and out the front doors, and Martha would have been perfectly delighted to talk to every single person for fifteen or twenty minutes each. We eventually reminded Martha that we had to be at the cemetery in an hour so we couldn't really extend the visitation time until, well, *Tuesday*—which meant that she needed to try her best to keep the conversations short and sweet. Asking Martha to aim for "short and sweet" is sort of like asking a fish to walk a little faster, but apparently the Lord is still in the business of miracles. We left the church with about ten minutes to spare.

Martha's one wish for Sissie's funeral was for someone to sing Sissie's favorite hymn at the graveside service. She asked the Johnson children—three Myrtlewood teenagers who meant the world to Martha and Sissie—if they'd be willing to sing an a cappella version of "Amazing Grace," and it thrilled her to no end when they agreed. Sissie's burial plot was at the top of a hill, right next to her late husband's, and as the pastor finished his remarks and closed the service with a prayer, the Johnsons stood on the side of the hill and sang out over the valley below:

Amazing grace! how sweet the sound—
That saved a wretch like me!
I once was lost but now am found,
Was blind but now I see.

'Twas grace that taught my heart to fear,
And grace my fears relieved;
How precious did that grace appear
The hour I first believed!

Through many dangers, toils and snares
I have already come;
'Tis grace hath brought me safe thus far,
And grace will lead me home.

When we've been there ten thousand years,
Bright shining as the sun,
We've no less days to sing God's praise
Than when we'd first begun.

143

As the last note trailed away, Martha turned to Rose and me and said, "Have you ever heard anything more perfectly beautiful? Was that not perfectly beautiful? It was just perfectly beautiful!" And Martha was right. The service *was* perfectly beautiful, a wonderful tribute to 101 well-lived years.

And even though we miss her like crazy, our family is so fortunate to have the peace of knowing that Sissie is with Jesus now. She's free to run and dance and rake to her heart's content. And while I don't know for sure, I strongly suspect that her bangs are holding up just beautifully. I bet her hair even stays set when it gets wet.

It's part of her heavenly inheritance.

Lord be praised.

CHAPTER SIXTEEN

Because Nothing Says "Happy Anniversary" like Eight Pounds of Bacon

SEEING AS HOW I was a late-in-life baby who arrived almost a full decade after the sibling before me, I was only nine years old when my parents celebrated their twenty-fifth wedding anniversary. Chox and Joe hosted a party to commemorate the occasion, and while I don't remember much about the night, I do remember that my mama very elegantly held the same glass of wine for approximately three hours. Mama doesn't drink—she has always contended that she's allergic to alcohol, that even the smallest amount makes her fingers go numb and therefore renders her incapable of cutting her food—but that night somebody handed her a glass of wine, and since she didn't want to be rude or appear wasteful, she walked around and visited with her and Daddy's friends, all the while cradling the base of that wine glass like she was waiting for a congregant to dip some bread in it for Communion.

Eventually she was able to discreetly dispose of the warm

wine in Chox's sink, and for that we're all quite grateful. Because believe me, if Mama thought there was the slightest chance she was going to hurt anyone's feelings by pouring her wine down the drain, she would have cradled that glass for the remainder of my childhood.

I'm not kidding. That glass of wine would have gone to my high school graduation. Might have even made it to my wedding.

You may be picking up on the fact that people pleasing runs deep on that side of the family. I come by it honestly.

Since I was just a bystander at Mama and Daddy's twenty-fifth anniversary (well, a bystander and a copious mental-note taker, apparently), it was strange to find myself in the role of party planner when it was time to celebrate their fiftieth. Sister, Brother, and I agreed that a celebration was most definitely in order, so Sister, Janie, and I took the party bull by the horns.

We wanted to make sure we gave the milestone the attention and care it deserved, but at the same time we didn't want to do anything that Mama and Daddy would consider overly fancy. Since Daddy detests the slightest hint of pretense and Mama would rather be with family and close friends than just about anything else on earth, it didn't take long for us to decide that a dinner at Brother and Janie's house in Memphis was the way to go. We set the date, sent out the invitations, and planned the menu, and the Wednesday before the party (which was to take place on Saturday evening), I loaded my car and drove to Memphis. David and the little guy would join me a couple of days later, but until then, I had a whole lot of grocery shopping and prep work to do. Not to mention panicking.

I'm not an organized person by any stretch of the imagination, but whenever I face a process that has more than, say, five steps, I become a hypercompulsive list maker. The fear of leaving out some critical piece of the logistical puzzle prompts me to write and revise and type and revise and cross out and revise until the list is thorough and comprehensive and completely and utterly annoying to anyone besides me. I like to think my obsessive lists are part of my winsome charm, but really that's just a lie I tell myself in order to justify my fondness for the sight of a clean, sans serif font, double-spaced and appropriately numbered (maybe even alphabetized!) list on a piece (correction: pieces) of white paper.

You may be thinking that I need to get out more.

And I'm totally fine with getting out more as long as I can take Microsoft Word with me.

When I was a junior in college, my friends Marion, Tracey, Katy, and I decided to go to Washington, DC, for spring break. I wish I could remember what prompted such an unconventional choice—especially since the rest of our friends were going to Fort Walton Beach in Florida—but we were gung-ho about traveling to our nation's capital. Our parents were immediately on board with our plans ("You say you'd like to spend spring break visiting museums and historical monuments? Stopping by the Library of Congress? Taking a tour of the White House? Learning more about our country? LET ME WRITE YOU A CHECK"), and a travel agent in Starkville helped us find plane tickets. Since we read newspapers back then, I actually saw an ad in *USA Today* for a great hotel that was running a spring special, and our room ended up being super affordable.

Once we were all set in terms of getting there, I apparently needed a new problem to tackle and grew increasingly concerned that we'd arrive in DC and squander our time. I was afraid we'd sleep late every morning and wind up staring at the Washington Monument for ten seconds and calling it a day. In retrospect, I'd tell myself, *LIGHTEN UP, MAMAW—YOU'RE TWENTY YEARS OLD*, but for whatever reason, the prospect of having five days in DC and not making the most of the time was a completely unacceptable option to me.

I countered my apprehension by going to the bookstore when I was home in Myrtlewood one weekend and buying a copy of the Frommer's guide to Washington, DC. Then I sat down at my daddy's computer and came up with an itinerary for our trip. I typed out everything in WordPerfect, and when I finally came up for air three or four hours later and ripped off the tabs on the printouts from Daddy's sah-weet dot matrix printer, what I had created wasn't so much an itinerary as a travel manifesto.

It still makes me a little giddy when I think about it.

Fortunately, the DC manifesto served us well. We made some incredible memories, and we still laugh hysterically when we talk about how Tracey wore a red, white, and blue outfit—with matching hair bow, no less—to tour the White House. *Without a hint of irony.*

I am also pleased to report we didn't miss a single monument.

When it came to planning Mama and Daddy's anniversary party, all my list-making training from the DC trip came in handy. Oh, I'd had several opportunities to make equally extensive lists over the years, but the anniversary list was special because it incorporated groceries, a prep schedule for the food, a setup schedule for the party, and a pre-party cooking schedule so we knew when to put what dishes on the stove or in the oven.

I'm not gonna lie. It was spectacular.

Janie and Brother couldn't resist teasing me about it—it was five pages long, packed with asterisks, addendums, and codicils, and just a hair shy of being notarized—but considering my brain isn't terribly detail oriented, that list was the only thing standing between me and a complete pre-party meltdown. Plus, it reminded me that my first order of party business on Thursday morning was to GET THEE TO THE GROCERY STORE.

And that's exactly what I did. I loaded two carts to overflowing before you could say, "This celebratory meal appears to be somewhat high in trans fats," and once I'd hauled everything back to Brother and Janie's house, I tried as best as I could to arrange all the cans and boxes in the order we'd need them. Ironically, Mama is the first person I think to call when I'm in a situation where I need to organize a pantry or a refrigerator or a cabinet in a way that will make cooking more efficient and less frustrating, so I really could have used her help that afternoon.

(She minored in home economics in college, but personally I think she must have earned an added emphasis in food storage somewhere along the way.)

(Assuming food storage is, in fact, a recognized area of study.)

Regardless, when I contrast Mama's methodical, sensible placement of her groceries with my willy-nilly slinging of various and sundry food items, I can't help but wonder if I need to put a sign on my forehead that says, "WELCOME TO CRAZYTOWN. THE CUCKOO IS HERE AND ALSO IN MY PANTRY."

Once the groceries were situated, the first thing on our prep list was to mix the marinade for the beef tenderloin my brother was going to cook on the grill, and Janie and I managed to cross that item off our list late Thursday afternoon. Afterward we talked about what appetizers would work best, and Janie, who is *super* organized, ran through the list of everything we needed to do on Friday, then pulled out all the serving pieces that we'd need for Saturday night's dinner.

That evening Janie's mother, Jane (who, interestingly enough, I call Beverly, which might seem weird unless you consider that she calls me Stephanie, and as a result we crack each other up every time we say hello or good-bye), came by to check on our progress. She suggested that we label each serving piece with a Post-it note to remind us what dish would go inside—a tip I considered pretty much genius. My brain started to feel a little less cluttered and overwhelmed, and by the time I went to bed Thursday night, I was optimistic and hopeful about Friday. FIRE UP THE STOVE, GLADYS.

Friday morning was all about the side dishes, and that is precisely why I was cooking twelve boxes of Uncle Ben's Long Grain & Wild Rice by seven thirty in the morning. We were expecting about fifty people at the dinner—family members, close friends, former neighbors who had moved away years ago—and when I'd gone to the grocery store the day before, I was fighting an underlying fear that somehow we wouldn't have enough food. The fear caused me to buy about four more of everything than I initially thought we needed, but I figured it was better to miscalculate on the side of plenty rather than want. One of our dishes was a shrimp and wild-rice casserole, and while I probably ended up making enough for seventy-five people, at least I could rest easy knowing that, say, Mama's friend Betty Bailey wasn't going to walk up to the buffet table and find one whole teaspoon of casserole for her enjoyment. Heaven forbid.

While the rice was cooking, we started the arduous task of grating an obscene amount of cheese, and as I was attempting to calculate exactly how many calories were represented in our econo-sized blocks of cheddar, my dear friend Bubba rang the doorbell. Bubba and I have been friends since we were freshmen at State, and from the second we were introduced, we were like long-lost brother and sister. We put countless miles on our vehicles driving around Starkville, singing our hearts out, and talking until we were hoarse. We adored each other in the sweetest, most uncomplicated way. And we still do.

Bubba had the audacity to transfer to another college when we were juniors—he needed to be at a school that was better for his major—but that just meant we did most of our talking over the phone instead of in one of our cars. In the twenty-plus years we've known each other, Bubba has managed to endear himself to my whole family, and he has become friends with Sister and Barry as well as Brother and Janie. Even now I know I could call Bubba right this second, tell him I need him to be at my house tonight at seven, and he'd invoke my family nickname and say, "Well, hold on, Peaches—you're going to have to give me a few minutes to clear my calendar. It'll take me a little while to drive from Memphis to Birmingham, but I'll be there. What do you need me to bring?"

So when Bubba showed up to visit that Friday morning at Brother and Janie's house, it was hardly a surprise. After he hugged Janie and me within an inch of our lives, he grabbed a Coke from the refrigerator and settled onto one of the bar stools. It took approximately four seconds for him to make fun of the sheer quantity of cheese we were grating, but in true Bubba fashion, he followed up his teasing by saying, "So. What can I do to help?"

Since we were planning to serve a green-bean dish that's one of our family's favorites despite the fact that any green beans participating in said dish are left with absolutely no nutritional value, we wanted to go ahead and assemble the ingredients so the beans would have plenty of time to absorb all the flavors. It's one of those recipes where the green beans are more of a *vessel*, really—they're just a means for delivering the sweet-salty-bacony goodness to your mouth. Hallelujah.

We were making six batches of the beans, and while I can see how that might seem excessive, I know from personal experience that the green-bean recipe has a way of turning people into buzzards who will swoop in for seconds and thirds. That meant we needed to fry three pounds of bacon for the beans, and since we didn't want to skimp, we decided to add an additional pound for good measure. Plus, we needed four more pounds of bacon for assorted appetizers and our salad. Which would be eight pounds total. EIGHT POUNDS O'BACON.

Glory to God.

I don't know if I'd ever given any real consideration to how long it would take to fry eight pounds of bacon, but it's fair to say that this level of bacon frying requires a significant time commitment. Janie has a big stove, so she, Bubba, and I each commandeered the skillet or Dutch oven of our choosing, and y'all, we stood at that stove for over an hour and a half. It was surprisingly challenging to figure out how much each pan would take without turning the bacon into a chewy mess, and once I knew my skillet could handle five strips at a time—NO MORE—I settled into a rhythmic bacon-frying routine: add strips, wait, flip, wait, flip one more time, wait, move bacon to paper towels, pour grease into bowl, repeat.

As you can tell, it was all very glamorous.

Honestly, I felt like Bubba and I took our friendship to another level during those one hundred or so minutes. If I were at all crafty, which I'm not, I might have made him a commemorative plaque: *A friend loveth at all times, and a brother is born to helpeth you fryeth all the bacon. Amen.*

The next two days were a bit of a blur, but that is understandable since we were, as one of Daddy's cousins would say, busier than a one-armed paper hanger. Janie and I concentrated on moving through our manifesto/to-do list to finish preparing the food while Sister worked her magic, creating gorgeous flower arrangements to scatter around the house. (If I didn't know better, I would harbor suspicions that Sister is somehow related to Martha Stewart, because the things she can do with flowers— my word.)

Brother tended to the grill and cooked twenty pounds of beef tenderloin to absolute perfection. Barry and David must have made six trips around town to help with last-minute errands. And much to our relief (and maybe even surprise), by six o'clock Saturday night we were officially ready for the party. All we were missing were the people.

There were lots of times in my childhood when I thought my parents seemed like an odd match, when I wondered why Mama hadn't married somebody who was really outgoing like she is or why Daddy hadn't married somebody who was more introverted and serious like he is. I dwelled more on their differences than their similarities, and as a result I probably spent more time than was normal wondering if they were happy, if they were going to stay together, if they struggled to find stuff to talk about when the kids were away and they were the only two people in the house.

My tendency to worry unnecessarily has been a theme in my life since I was about six years old, and I think in the instance of my parents' marriage, this tendency was fueled by one too many after-school specials about divorce as well as some movie I saw one time about a girl whose parents split up and the mama couldn't get out of bed long enough to braid her daughter's hair in the mornings. For the sake of perspective, I should probably admit that I also had an unusual fear of dying in a Jet Ski accident after seeing a particularly harrowing episode of *All My Children* where Jenny Gardner tries out a Jet Ski on Willow Lake and then BLOWS SLAP UP while her brother, Tad, and her boyfriend, Greg, watch helplessly from the shore.

So I think it's fair to say that my fears haven't always been logical. Or, you know, based on anything even remotely resembling reality.

I wasted all manner of my teenage time and energy wanting to give Mama and Daddy the latest "Are You Sure You're Compatible?" quiz from *Seventeen* magazine and trying to think of hobbies they might enjoy participating in together. But as I've gotten older, I've realized that Mama and Daddy have always shared a quality that is absolutely invaluable when it comes to matters of marriage: commitment. Both of them are just rock solid in that regard. I've never known either one of them to start something without finishing it—or to make a promise and then break it. Just typing that makes me teary eyed, because MY GOODNESS, what a legacy that is.

And here's what I know now that I didn't know way back when: the Lord has used their commitment to each other—which has been unwavering, even when they were so frustrated with each other they could barely speak—to shape them and change them and mold them in ways that I don't think either of them could have anticipated. I recently read a quote by Elisabeth Elliot where she remarked that God "is always doing something—the very best thing, the thing we ourselves would certainly choose if we knew the end from the beginning. He is at work to bring us to our full glory." When I look at Mama and Daddy's marriage, I absolutely see evidence of that. Mama has mellowed my admittedly type-A daddy and helped him to be more compassionate and loving. Daddy has modeled consistency and steadiness to Mama and protected her from her natural inclination to be overly trusting and a little bit gullible. They balance and complement each other. It didn't happen overnight, but they really are more fully themselves than they were on their wedding day, than they were at their twenty-fifth anniversary, than they were last week, even.

And though the dynamics of our marriages are somewhat different from Mama and Daddy's, my sister, my brother, and I are impacted every single day by our parents' commitment, by their willingness to do the hard thing and trust that God's long-term plan for their marriage and their lives far outweighs any short-term tension or hurt or conflict.

I think it's safe to speak for the group and say that we are unspeakably grateful for that example.

🌷

There have been many instances in my life when the anticipation of an event turned out better than the event itself. And honestly I was a little concerned that that might be the case with Mama and Daddy's fiftieth anniversary party. We wanted more than anything to honor and esteem them in the presence of friends and family, but there's just no way to predict how a group dynamic will play out. Plus, if you're anything like me, a worst-case scenario sometimes lurks in the back of your mind, so I spent two or three days trying to block out visions of burning food, awkward silences, and unexpected no-shows.

155

(I'm telling you: I can get bound up in the fear and the worry.)

(In fact, one of my grad school professors once told me that my lamentations about the inadequacy of a paper I was working on made Jeremiah look like a stand-up comic.)

But Debbie Downer here need not have worried. The whole night—from the time the first guests arrived until we served the green beans with all that bacon until all the cousins moved out onto the patio and talked into the wee hours of the morning— was absolutely wonderful. Anyone who questions the power of consistent, humble, servant-hearted influence should have seen Mama and Daddy surrounded by their children, grandchildren, siblings, cousins, nieces, nephews, and longtime friends. An abundance—an overflow—of love, gratitude, and laughter filled Brother and Janie's house that night, all because a couple of people stood at the front of Moss Rose United Methodist Church and made a promise to God and to each other fifty years before.

That'll preach.

The next morning our immediate family met at Brother and Janie's for a quick breakfast before everybody hit the road. Our little guy was whiny and tired from being up late the night before, and asking him to do anything other than sit in his grandmother's lap resulted in a fresh crop of tears. My younger nephew, Houston, was running around the kitchen in a Transformers costume, trying his best to convince Janie that miniature M&M's were a fine and nutritious breakfast, while my older nephew, Beck, tried his level best to convince Mama that what she *really* wanted to do was make him a fresh batch of pancakes. Sister was nursing a killer migraine thanks to a weather front that was threatening to move through the Mid-South later that afternoon, and while she turned a deeper shade of green with every passing minute, I was trying to pack our bags in a hurry so we could get back to Birmingham in time to pick up our dogs at the kennel.

That calm, serene, laid-back vibe from the night before was nowhere to be found. It felt like a distant memory, like it *might* have happened somewhere around the time of the Eisenhower administration, but certainly not within the previous twenty-four hours. No way.

But that's family. They're the people who make you willing—eager, even—to drive four and a half hours so you can spend three days in the kitchen and fry eight pounds of bacon (or cook twenty pounds of beef or arrange six dozen flowers) for one night of celebration that's followed by a morning mired in the depths. And you do it so that someday, maybe fifteen or twenty years down the road, you can think back on an anniversary party, tell your children or grandchildren about it, and say, with all sincerity, "My word. That was a gift. That whole thing was a gift."

Because that's family. That's what you do. That's how you love.

And you know what?

It *is* a gift.

Every single bit of it.

CHAPTER SEVENTEEN

It Only Takes a Spark to Get a Kindle Going

ONE OF THE ADVANTAGES of growing up in a smallish town is that if you end up marrying someone who is from that same smallish town, odds are you will have known each other's family members for what feels like forever. When I was in elementary school, for example, it never occurred to me that Martha, the sweet lady in my parents' Sunday school class, might one day be my mother-in-law, or that Scott, the always-smiling friend of my brother's, would be my brother-in-law, or that Rose, the pretty homecoming queen who was Scott's high school girlfriend, would be my sister-in-law.

But sure enough, when David and I started dating and then got engaged and then got married, becoming part of his family was an easy transition because, well, I'd known everybody since I'd been a kid running through Mission Hill United Methodist Church with Popsicle smeared all over my face. So for me, an added bonus to saying, "I do" was that I would share a last name with people I had known and loved for a big chunk of my life.

(That was sort of sweet, wasn't it?)

(Well, it ought to be. Because I mean it.)

Since I'd known David's family for so long, I was already well aware that a long-standing practice with the Hudsons is that David is the go-to person for any questions or issues related to electronics. Actually, he's the go-to person for any questions or issues related to Items with a Switch or a Plug, and I never realized how much Martha and Sissie depended on him for small repairs and whatnot until our first post-wedding visit to Myrtlewood. We pulled in the driveway, ready for a home-cooked meal and a piece of Martha's Italian cream cake, only to find Sissie standing at the carport door with a couple of boxes of lightbulbs in her hands.

For the first fifteen minutes of our visit David trailed behind his grandmother while she walked from room to room and pointed out overhead lights that needed to be changed. We did eventually get to enjoy a home-cooked meal and Italian cream cake, too—but David had to work for it first. And for the next ten years, every single visit to Martha and Sissie's house followed that same pattern.

It was never just lightbulbs, though; Martha and Sissie shared a disdain for all things involving buttons. As a result, David often had to set the time on the coffeepot, adjust the color on the living room TV, program the preset stations on Martha's car stereo, or set the speed-dial options on the cordless phone. Really, it didn't matter if it was a flashlight or a cell phone; Martha and Sissie would see buttons and immediately throw up their hands in resignation.

🌹

To be fair, Martha has more than earned the right to be frustrated with buttons and plugs and the like. She is unwavering in her belief that THINGS SHOULD JUST WORK, but her personal experience tells a different story, I'm afraid. In the mid

'70s David's daddy, Dan, bought Martha a Buick that could only be described as "gigantor." Martha had test-driven several cars, including one she claimed smelled like rotten eggs, so at first the Buick with the new-car smell was a huge hit.

Eventually, however, there was the none-too-small matter that the Buick didn't like to stop running when Martha turned it off. She'd ease into the carport, put the Buick in park, then cut the ignition, but that big ole sedan was stubborn. The motor would continue to chug and sputter and spit as Martha gathered her belongings from the car and walked into the house, so she usually sidestepped to the back door while nervously looking over her shoulder, trying to avoid being startled by the final *THUMP* or *BOOM* from the engine. Martha also maintained that the car made a noise like "those whirlybirds on that ride at the fair! You know that whirlybird ride at the fair? I could drive for five or six blocks, and then all of a sudden it sounded like those whirlybirds were trapped underneath the hood of the car! Like they were chirpin' and whistlin' and carryin' on like that whirlybird ride at the fair!"

And if Martha happened to be at, say, the Winn-Dixie when the Buick decided to show out, you'd better believe Dan would hear all about it. Even now Martha will recount the horrors of being in the Winn-Dixie parking lot when "all I wanted was to talk to my friend Regina! I just wanted to talk to Regina! Because I'd be in the parking lot and see her walking into the Winn-Dixie, and I'd say, 'Regina! Hey, Regina!' but she couldn't hear a word I was saying because that car—THAT CAR—was still going, *POP POP, VROOOOOOM, CLANK, POP POP*, and there was no way Regina could have heard me, there was just no way—not in the middle of all that racket!"

After a few years Martha finally convinced Dan to trade in the Buick, and since Dan had recently read Lee Iacocca's autobiography, he was more resolved than ever to buy another American vehicle, which meant Dan came home one day with a brand-new Chrysler Fifth Avenue—a trade that did absolutely nothing to alleviate Martha's vehicular exasperation. In fact, the fully loaded Fifth Avenue brought with it a whole new assortment of problems, including but not limited to a door handle that would often fall off the driver's side door. Martha never got out of that car without wondering if she'd be able to get back into it, and I certainly can't blame her. Having a door handle that actually stays attached to the door seems like a small request where matters of car maintenance are concerned.

That Fifth Avenue, for all its fancy buttons and levers, left Martha more convinced than ever that an array of bells and whistles might look real pretty on a display, but the reality of it all was that they were too high maintenance for her. Unfortunately, there wasn't one thing Martha could do to turn the advancing technological tide when it came to cars and TVs and phones and, well, *everything*. So by the time the Internet took off in the mid to late '90s, Martha was out of her depth completely. That fact was totally evident when, after David ordered a gift for her online and had it shipped to her house, she called us with an exciting announcement.

"Sophie? I just wanted to let you know that I just got my package! I just got it! It's from Amazon-dot-C-zero-M! It's from Amazon-dot-C-zero-M!"

God love her. I didn't have the heart to tell her that there aren't any zeros in *.com*. Mainly because she wouldn't have known what in the world *.com* is. Or that Amazon doesn't really have anything to do with the jungle.

And I guess that's sort of my point.

After the Amazon-dot-C-zero-M phone call, David recognized there was going to be a steep learning curve not too far down the road, so he devised a Martha Technology Strategy (MTS) that served us pretty well for a few years. The MTS was to try to avoid introducing Martha to any new technology, while helping her navigate whatever technology she couldn't escape. So when (true story) she called us to complain that her TV was turning on in the middle of the night at full volume, David walked her through the steps to disable the timer. When (true story) lightning hit that same TV a few years later, David helped her pick out a new one that would be easy for her to operate. When (true story) she bought her very first foreign car, a Honda Accord, in 2002, David showed her how to load six CDs into her stereo.

Which means (true story) that she has been listening to a steady rotation of Kenny G, Frank Sinatra, and Elvis Presley for well over a decade.

Managing the MTS has been trickier over the last six or seven years, though—no doubt about it. Once I started a blog, for example, Martha mentioned that she'd love to have a way to read it, and there were several times when David and I debated giving her one of our computers or buying her a device that would enable her to set up an e-mail account and read whatever blogs she wanted via e-mail subscriptions. Inevitably, though, the discussion would come to a screeching halt when David would pose a critical question: *So, if we do this—who's going to be Martha's tech support person?*

And that question? It would shut everything down.

SHUT.

IT.

DOWN.

163

After all, we'd learned the hard way that even the best-intentioned MTS requires tech support, and considering David has spent hours—HOURS—on the phone over the last fifteen years trying to explain how to reset the time on the VCR ("David? The display just says HH-MM! It just says HH-MM! And I can't make it stop saying HH-MM!") or how to unlock the oven from the self-cleaning setting or how to answer a cell phone without hanging up on the caller, we knew that introducing Martha to a computer or an iPad was beyond his tech-support capabilities. We wished the circumstances were different, but there was no way to ignore the cold, hard truth: MTS is a full-time job.

For a while it looked like Rose's mother, Julia Claire, had come to the MTS rescue. Julia Claire owns a real live computer, and she offered to pull up some of my old blog posts and print them out for Martha. Martha was skeptical about whether or not the plan would work, primarily because, in Martha's words, "I'm pretty sure Julia Claire's computer is just for ordering things! It's only for ordering things!" Fortunately, though, Julia Claire's computer also worked for surfing the Internet, and she was able to print off four or five blog posts for Martha to read. It was an MTS victory, but alas, it was short term. Martha ultimately decided she didn't want to waste all Julia Claire's printer paper and really, since Julia Claire mainly used the computer for ordering things! just for ordering things!, Martha didn't want to impose and ask for weekly blog printouts.

Hey there, MTS square one. Nice to see you again.

For the next couple of years Martha stayed in a technological holding pattern. But last fall, in what David and I considered to be a stroke of genius as well as the possible answer to all of our MTS prayers, Scott and Rose decided to give Martha a Kindle for Christmas. We figured a Kindle would be the easiest of all devices for her to manage because there are only a couple of buttons, a charger, and a black-and-white screen, so essentially it's only slightly more complicated than a bag phone.

Not that Martha ever mastered the use of a bag phone, mind you. But still. The idea had some real promise.

The Friday before Christmas we drove to Myrtlewood to celebrate with the Hudson side of the family, and Rose suggested that we have our Christmas lunch at the country club since she and Martha both had been cooking nonstop for open houses and neighborhood parties and Sunday school gatherings. My parents have never been members of the country club, thanks to my daddy's long-standing belief that he shouldn't have to pay somebody money for the privilege of paying them even more money, but even he admits that the country club in Myrtlewood has some of the best food in town. The chicken salad plate with fresh fruit and tiny pimento-cheese sandwiches is one of those dishes that screams, *This is home* to me, and sure enough, that's exactly what Martha ordered when we sat down for our Christmas meal. The rest of the table was a study in fried Southern goodness—fried oysters, fried catfish, fried chicken—and as is almost always the case when we're with Scott and Rose and their daughter, Melissa, our time at lunch was easy and good. They're a laid-back bunch, and getting to hang out with them always makes my heart happy.

It's nice to be able to say that about family, you know?

After lunch we went back to Martha's to exchange gifts, which meant it wouldn't be long until the Unveiling of the Kindle. David and I nearly derailed the proceedings when we gave Martha a poncho that I'd found for her at Stein Mart, but after she got the poncho pirouetting and posing out of her system, Martha finally sat down to open her gift from Scott and Rose. David and I felt invested in her reaction to the Kindle—in fact, part of our gift to her was an Amazon account with a credit so she could start her collection of e-books—so we were hopeful as we witnessed the launch of MTS 2.0. It was just like Steve Jobs must have felt on the day Apple launched the iPhone. Except I'm pretty positive the first iPhone wasn't operated by a five-foot-one-inch grandmother who owns approximately fifty-three three-quarter-sleeve jackets in varying shades of green.

When Martha finally opened her gift and saw the Kindle box, her reaction was more than any of us had imagined. She was thrilled, and as she carefully examined the box, she said, "Oh! You just don't know! You just don't know how I've wanted one of these! Because so many of the girls have one! And they all say they're wonderful! Just perfectly wonderful! And I'm going to read and be so cute and so fun and I'm just going to enjoy it!" We were all happy to see her so enthusiastic, but at the same time we knew that enthusiasm was only half the battle.

Because somebody was going to have to teach her how to use that Kindle. And nobody was volunteering.

Martha had just started to dig through the box for (non-existent) instructions when David noticed that the "perfectly darling" red case Scott and Rose had bought for the Kindle was actually a case for a Nook. This discovery sent Martha into a chorus of, "Oh, you don't mean! Do you mean it? You don't mean!" and put a big, fat exclamation point at the end of Martha's lifelong assertion that she has the worst luck in the world and every time she finds a cute top the store doesn't have her size and whenever she finds a lipstick color that she likes it's immediately discontinued and if she parks in the most remote spot at Dollar General her car will still get nicked by a shopping cart and she just can't have anything because something always goes wrong and it only happens to her, do you see?

Do you see how it always happens to her?

Something always goes wrong!

Scott and David know all too well that when Martha starts to get wound up about the dire misfortune of a missing button or a humming air conditioner or an oddly placed electrical outlet, the best course of action is to keep calm and come up with a plan— preferably one that can be implemented quickly. Scott wisely suggested that we make a quick trip to Best Buy to get a new case, and I for one thought that was an excellent idea, especially since I'd been tinkering with Martha's Kindle during the discussion about the wrong case and realized it was the wrong Kindle, too. Martha needed a 3G Kindle since she doesn't have Wi-Fi at home (nor does she have DSL or a cable modem or one of those old-timey modems that cradles the phone receiver), so yes, going to Best Buy was a fantastic plan. Top notch. Crank 'er up.

Thankfully the exchange process at Best Buy was quick and merciful, and we would have been in and out of the store within five minutes save the small, surprising detail that Rose decided to buy a TV for Julia Claire while we were there. I recognize that the impromptu TV purchase might seem unusual to some, but it was a total Rose move. Rose rarely spends money on anything besides groceries and gasoline—she'd rather play tennis or run or work in her yard than participate in a big day of shopping—so when she buys something, she moves fast and decisively, trying to keep the purchase as painless as possible.

She's a straight shooter with no interest in haggling or bargaining; she just wants to get the shopping over with and hurry back to the tennis court, for the love of Pete. That's why none of us were surprised when she took time to pick out a forty-two-inch television when presumably we were only at the Best Buy to return Martha's Kindle. It was a perfect way for Rose to check off

"Get Mama's Christmas gift" from her list without having to take away one second from the next week's outdoor activities. Buying the TV wasn't impulsive; it was efficient. Classic Rose.

On the way back to Martha's we stopped by Scott and Rose's house to use their computer so we could double-check Martha's Amazon account and set up her new 3G Kindle. Somehow I ended up being the person in charge of all Kindle-related duties, and honestly, I was a little surprised that my own husband—the man who is my very best friend and, if you want to get down-right biblical about it, is supposed to love me as Christ loves the church—threw me to the MTS 2.0 wolves so quickly. When I was typing Martha's account information into the Kindle, I grinned at David and said, "Seriously? You're just going to sit there and let me do this? Since when did I become the point person for all things Amazon?"

He shook his head. "I know it's a lot to take on," he answered, "but honestly, I don't have the strength for this one. Because remember when she moved? And she wanted the phone in her garage? And she talked for two days about how her friend Gertrude has a phone in her garage and it's just so fun because the girls like to sit in the garage and visit and when the phone rings it's just right there! It's just right there by the door! And you don't have to go inside to answer it! Do you remember that? Do you remember how long it took me to explain that I was not in fact an employee of the phone company and therefore could not install a phone jack in her garage? Do you remember how hard I tried to make her understand that if she wanted a phone in her garage, then maybe she should just TAKE HER CORDLESS PHONE OUTSIDE?"

I laughed, nodded sympathetically, and he sighed.

"Well, it nearly did me in," he continued. "So while I'm happy to help with the Kindle stuff if you need it, and while

I'll offer all sorts of moral support, I'd be mighty grateful if you could take this one for the team."

In that moment, I understood. By default David had served as Martha's electronic troubleshooter and repairman for almost forty years. He'd examined malfunctioning power locks, stubborn cable cords, and countless blinking clock radios. Now that Martha was going to have a device that would enable her to purchase books, download books, and subscribe to blogs—NOW THAT THE INTERNET WAS INVOLVED—he recognized the magnitude of the task at hand. And he needed a break.

I sat quietly for a minute and pondered what the Lord might be calling me to do in this particular situation. Maybe He simply wanted me to be my husband's tech support helpmeet. Maybe He wanted me to be Martha's IT person for such a time as this. Maybe He wanted me to be a Ruth to Martha's Naomi, and wherever Martha's Kindle would go, I would go. Wherever Martha's Kindle would stay, I would stay.

Or maybe He wanted me to dial down the overspiritualizing a notch or ten and finish adding the account information to the Kindle so my mother-in-law could start enjoying her Christmas present already.

So that's exactly what I did.

🌷

About thirty minutes later the Kindle was operational and secure in its sassy new case. We drove back to Martha's house, and as I prepared to show her how to use the Kindle, six words ran on a loop in my brain:

Be near, Lord Jesus. Be near.

The next hour proved to be one of the most memorable of my life. Martha, bound and determined to figure out the Kindle, cemented her status as an auditory learner. She repeated every single word I said.

"Martha, this is the home screen."

"This is the home screen!"

"Martha, this is your list of downloaded books."

"This is the list of downloaded books!"

"Martha, this is your shopping cart."

"This is the shopping cart!"

I don't know when I've encountered a more eager student. And when I showed her how to tap the edges of the screen in order to turn pages, she was all over it. She hit the side of that Kindle like a buzzer, raising herself halfway off the couch and exclaiming, "Turn the page! TURN THE PAGE!"

If I'd had a medal, I would've draped it around her neck right then and there, proclaimed her the Kindle champion, led her to the top of a platform, and played a recording of the national anthem. It was Martha's Technological Moment in Time, and she was giddy with progress.

However, when Martha's Kindle coach (that would be me) returned to Birmingham the night of our tutorial, Martha lost her Kindle confidence. She tried to recapture it by taking her Kindle to the Best Buy and asking for help there. She was incredulous that there was no on-site Kindle tech support, so she called me. "Can you believe they don't service the Kindles?" she asked. "And they don't offer lessons? They don't offer lessons at the Best Buy!" Martha then beseeched the local public library for help, where "there was the nicest young man there! Just the nicest young man! But he didn't know anything about Kindles!" I tried as best I could to talk her through questions on the phone, but doing that meant we had to fight our way through a technological language barrier.

The next few weeks passed without incident, but at the end

of January, Martha called and said, "Now, Sophie, if I click that little thingy at the bottom of the screen—well, I mean, I don't really click it because it doesn't click, I just sort of mash it, not real hard or anything, I just sort of push it, really—but if I sort of push that button and then wait maybe one, maybe two seconds, shouldn't I be able to see that list with all that stuff I can do? You know, that list with all that stuff I can do?"

"Ma'am?"

"Well, I don't really know how to explain it to you, but I'm trying to get to that list with all the stuff. Not the instruction manual. But the list with the stuff. The list with the stuff! How do I get to the list with the stuff?"

All I knew to say was, "Martha, I'm not sure."

But what I wanted to say was, "Martha, you may need to make a trip to the Books-A-Million and buy some real books with some real pages. ASAP."

I give Martha all the credit in the world, though. Trying to learn how to use the Kindle must have driven her absolutely crazy, but she never wavered in her commitment to it. Every time we talked, she told me how much she was enjoying it, how easy it was to read, how she could just sit in her bed late at night and "turn the page! TURN THE PAGE!" And it was fun! Just so much fun! It was more fun!

But the Amazon account we'd set up for her told a different tale. Martha hadn't ordered a new e-book since Christmas. When she mentioned it made her nervous to click "Buy" because she wasn't sure how Amazon was going to get their money, I promised her we'd taken care of those details. No matter what I said, though, I couldn't seem to assuage her concerns, and I wondered if the Kindle might find itself called into permanent service as a coaster on Martha's nightstand.

But finally—mercifully—a friend of Julia Claire's gave Martha some excellent, in-person Kindle pointers, and the pieces of the techy puzzle started to fit together for her. Lo and behold, early that next May, more than four months after the Kindle Christmas, my e-mail dinged with a notification that there'd been a purchase on Martha's Amazon account. She'd bought a Mary Higgins Clark novel—downloaded it and everything. I'm confident our neighbors must have heard me when I stuck my head in the hallway and yelled, "DAAAA-VID! You're not going to believe this! Martha just downloaded a book!"

"No way!" he answered.

"Way!" I replied. And then I laughed so hard I clapped my hands. If I'd been in Myrtlewood, I think I would've chest-bumped my mother-in-law. Gently. What with me being two of her and all.

Now that Martha has conquered the Kindle, I have high hopes that there's even more technology in her future. Who knows? She might even have an e-mail address sometime soon. She might upgrade to an iPad. She might buy a computer.

But make no mistake: if the extent of Martha's technological progress is that she downloads a Mary Higgins Clark book to her Kindle once a quarter, that's fine by us. Because while it may have taken fifteen years, downloading those books assures us of something that would have seemed impossible when David and I first married: Martha finally knows how to use the Amazon-dot-C-zero-M.

It's probably not a miracle, but it's close.

And now we just have to teach her how to set that clock on her coffeepot.

Be near, Lord Jesus.

Be near.

CHAPTER EIGHTEEN

That Whole Table Thing Is Pretty Symbolic, Y'all

LATE ONE AFTERNOON when Alex was seven years old, we were looking through one of my old photo albums when we ran across several family Easter pictures from the '70s and '80s. It was hilarious to see how Mama's and Chox's hairstyles evolved over the years—with my favorite being their sassy Mia Farrow–esque pixie cuts—and everybody's dress choices cut a wide fashion swath, to say the least. There were miniskirts, jersey ensembles, Laura Ashley florals, and Gunne Sax prairie dresses, along with some pleated, pearl-buttoned numbers from an Easter when Paige and I were clearly drawn to anything pastel and chiffon.

I blame our chiffon phase on watching too many reruns of *The Lawrence Welk Show*. Cissy's skirts always looked so pretty when she danced.

Taking an Easter picture was a nonnegotiable annual event in our family, and the backdrop was typically daffodils or azaleas, depending on which were in bloom at the time. Pictures always preceded Easter lunch, another annual event where Mama and Chox coordinated the food and alternated hosting duties. As kids we never knew who else might be joining us—it might be the minister of music or maybe some cousins or maybe even the preacher and his wife. Plus, Easter always meant that Sister and Brother would be home, and if Sister was home, that meant that she and Chox would exchange a seemingly endless supply of post-lunch stories that afternoon.

The food was great, but the stories and the laughter were always my favorite parts.

Over the last ten or fifteen years, there has been a little bit more of a rotation in terms of who might be in Myrtlewood for Easter. Mama and Daddy still sing in the choir, and Daddy still teaches Sunday school, so they're locked in at Mission Hill UMC every Easter. Their presence in my hometown is never in question. But all "the children" are grown now, and we have responsibilities at our own churches that sometimes make it difficult to travel Easter weekend. No matter who can be in Myrtlewood, Mama is always a little sad about the ones who can't be there, and a few years ago, when she was bemoaning the absence of some branch of the family, I reminded her that if her children *weren't* serving in their home churches, she'd be worried to death that she and Daddy had FAILED AT PARENTING.

She agreed, but that didn't change the fact that she wanted all her children around her table, just like it was back in the day when all the men in the family wore three-piece suits and ties so wide you'd swear they were napkins. Or like it was when I was nineteen and wore a floral skirt with a floral jacket and a floral shirt underneath. It would've been way too much floral if I hadn't neutralized the whole outfit with my neon-pink shoes.

Last spring Mama and Daddy both turned eighty within a

week of each other, and as I was driving back to Birmingham after a surprise birthday luncheon for Mama, something shifted in me. I tried my best to shake it, but that something kept reminding me that, as clichéd as it sounds, time is precious—and somehow, when I wasn't really paying attention, everybody got older. Honestly, I've never really paid much attention to the aging process; I'm a forty-two-year-old who feels about twenty-seven and tries not to devote much energy to counting all those pesky, crinkly lines around my eyes. In fact, I'm *still* shocked when someone asks my age and I have to say a number that is IN THE FORTIES, MY WORD. I keep my friends and family tucked away in the same little ageless bubble, but there's really no denying that the time, it is a-passin' when you've just celebrated your mother's eightieth birthday.

It gets your attention. For sure.

I've never had a midlife crisis, but that day, as I drove down the interstate, I think I had a midlife wake-up call. And what hit me—or smacked me in the face, to be honest—is that I really don't want to trade time with my parents for serving some pound cake at my church. I'm not saying I can't do both—of course, I can—but I am saying that over the course of the last seven or eight years, I fell into the trap of thinking that, as a grown-up, I was indispensable at my church and inconsequential around my parents' table.

And that's just not true. Neither of those things is true. I just got so busy doing what was good that I lost sight of what, at this particular stage in my life, might be better.

So last Easter we did things a little differently. My little family went to the early service at our church in Birmingham, and after church was over, we drove to my hometown for Easter lunch. Over the last few years we've gradually transitioned to having

Thanksgiving and Christmas at our house, but Mama and Chox still wanted to host Easter lunch in Myrtlewood. So instead of trying to convince Mama why she shouldn't go to any trouble and why she didn't need to wear herself out and why it would all be easier if she let everybody pick up food instead of trying to cook it herself and why and why and why, I just shut my mouth and showed up. And oh, was I ever glad I did.

As she has done all my life, Mama prepared a wonderful meal for us. Maybe it was because we'd just celebrated her eightieth birthday, but I found myself eyeing Mama like I was watching a movie, doing my best to take in her mannerisms and her expressions as she carefully stirred the contents of one pot and then the next, as she leaned down to check on the rolls in the oven, as she moved from one side of the kitchen to the other to make sure there was plenty of ice in the freezer. Her movements were more hesitant than they used to be, and she'd occasionally use the countertop to steady herself before pulling a platter from the cabinet or putting the iced tea in the refrigerator. Every once in a while she'd ask one of us to help her move a large dish to the buffet, but I thought it was pretty remarkable that Mama was still setting a gorgeous table and serving us so cheerfully—just a little more slowly than she used to.

Once everybody had fixed their plates and we settled in to the meal, I looked at all the children around Mama's kitchen table. My adorable nephews were at that age where even their weariness with adults (eye roll) who are, like, so lame (eye roll) because they still use words like *lame* (eye roll) and don't know any of their music (eye roll) and can barely operate an iPad (eye roll) still can't conceal a deep, underlying, pinch-their-cheeks sweetness. It thrills me to pieces to think about what they'll be doing in five or ten years, what God-given passions they'll be chasing. My cousin

Benji's girls are more beautiful every time I see them, and even though I want to put bricks on their respective heads to make them quit all that growing, they're kindhearted and quick witted, and they make friends faster than anyone I've ever known. Give those two a pool full of kids, and they'll find new BFFs in four minutes flat. I love that about them.

And then there's our little guy and Paige's little boy, Joseph. I like to call them Papaw and Scooter McGee, since Alex is a sixty-year-old man in a nine-year-old body and Joseph tends to operate at an energy level that can only be described as WIDE OPEN. They are polar opposites personality-wise but couldn't adore each other more. Papaw likes being responsible, following the rules, making a list and checking it twice. Scooter likes keeping his options open and charting his own course, often grabbing a guitar and singing some old Elvis songs just for kicks and grins. But both of them are full of life, full of wonder, and full of laughter. I'm so thankful for those little stinkers.

And what I know beyond a shadow of a doubt—at least when it comes to my husband and me, to my siblings, to my in-laws and cousins and friends—is that if our generation wants the phrase *legacy of faith* to mean anything at all to those kids around the table—if we want to go beyond spouting one more piece of Christian lingo that sounds real pretty but holds precious little significance in their lives—then we have to share our stories with them. We have to write them down, we have to say them out loud, we have to put away our phones and close our computers and linger at the table long after the meal is over. We have to make much of what God has done in our lives and what He continues to do.

After all, why in the world would we keep our firsthand experiences with His faithfulness, His grace, His kindness, His mercy, and His joy to ourselves?

As Papaw Davis used to say, "That don't even make good sense."

A few years ago I visited Nashville for a couple of days, mainly just to hang out with Sister and make the rounds to see a few friends. After two of the most relational days of my life—filled with loads of conversation and a week's worth of caffeine—I called my friend Angela on the way out of town and asked if I could stop by her house for a few minutes. My plan was to stay for half an hour, tops, and then get back on the road. No lolly-gagging.

Somehow, though, one conversational topic led to another and to another and to another, and around hour three of our visit, I mentioned to Angela that there was one particular area of my life where I felt completely numb, where I didn't know how to pray anymore because I was just tired all the way to my bones of dealing with that situation.

"I get it," Angela responded. "I really do."

We sat in silence for several seconds before she continued. "You know, one thing that always helps me when I'm struggling with what to pray or how to pray is to just remember. *Remember.*"

"Remember?" I asked.

"Yes. Remember. Actively remember the Lord's goodness. Say it out loud. Thank Him for what He's done for you in the past. Make a list of what you've seen Him do in your life. Speak it. REMEMBER."

Angela was right on target, of course, and somehow our attention turned to Psalm 77:11-15—a passage that couldn't have been timelier:

I will remember the deeds of the LORD;
    yes, I will remember your wonders of old.
I will ponder all your work,
    and meditate on your mighty deeds.
Your way, O God, is holy.
    What god is great like our God?
You are the God who works wonders;
    you have made known your might among the peoples.
You with your arm redeemed your people,
    the children of Jacob and Joseph.

Well. All righty then.

An hour or so later I managed to tear myself away from Angela's kitchen table so I could drive back to Birmingham. Once I navigated my way to I-65, I settled into the right lane, turned down my radio, and started talking to the Lord. Out loud.

Make no mistake. At first I felt as crazy as a Betsy bug. Cuckoo. I tried to tell myself that nobody was paying attention to me, that I really wasn't that conspicuous, but I still longed to grab a giant bullhorn, roll down my window, and scream, "Don't mind me, fellow travelers. I'm just cruising down the interstate, talking out loud and weeping openly, and YES, I REALIZE THAT YOU CANNOT IN FACT SEE ANYONE ELSE IN MY VEHICLE, BUT I PROMISE THAT GOD IS HERE, AND ALSO I AM REALLY VERY NORMAL."

Unfortunately there weren't any giant bullhorns available.

And what I realized fairly quickly was that I didn't need to worry about what people in other cars might be thinking. Because the more I talked, the more I remembered. And the more I remembered, the more I rested in the assurance that there has not been one instance in my life where God has left me or forsaken me. He has worked so intricately in the midst of my circumstances that it's almost impossible for me to comprehend His creativity as He moved me from point A to point B. But He somehow did it. He *is doing* it. He has saved me from myself over and over again. And somewhere around the Alabama line, the dam in my heart—the one built out of not really knowing how to pray and wondering if God even had a clue about how exhausted I was from dealing with that particular problem—well, it began to give way.

And listen. I'm not saying that the reason we need to actively remember what God has done is so we can all have a big, touchy-feely, emotional moment that makes us feel better for a day or two before we jump right back into the worry again. I'm not saying that at all. But I am saying that when we take time to see God's intention as He acts, His deliberate nature as He unfolds His plan, and His faithfulness as He watches after every detail of our lives, we're reminded of His character. We're reminded of His love for us. We're reminded of the truth of Psalm 143:5-6:

> I remember the days of old;
>> I meditate on all that you have done;
>> I ponder the work of your hands.
> I stretch out my hands to you;
>> my soul thirsts for you like a parched land.

We see evidence of His provision. We see the consistency of His care.

And that's what happened that afternoon in the car. I realized that IF HE ORDAINED ALL THAT STUFF I'M REMEM-BERING, HE HAS A PLAN FOR THIS STUFF, TOO. And He's writing a story that goes far beyond the here and now.

I knew that already, of course. I knew it in my head, at least. Somewhere along the way, though, frustration with the situation shifted my focus—and I'd forgotten it in my heart.

But then I remembered.

After Easter lunch was over, Paige and I served ice cream to the kids. They'd stayed in their seats at the table because, well, ICE CREAM, and as we scooped out Blue Bell Homemade Vanilla for the young'uns, Brother started talking about how different things had been when we were younger. He and Benji were laughing about some of their childhood mischief in Mamaw and Papaw's pasture—tales that always seem to involve a horse, a truck, or both—when Brother suddenly sat straight up in his chair and said, "Hey! Do y'all remember when we had a garbage man who was always at odds with the dogs on Mama and Daddy's road?"

Whether he meant to or not, he had instantly secured the undivided attention of every single child at the table.

"I have no idea what you're talking about," I said, looking over my shoulder as I carried another couple of dinner plates to the kitchen sink.

"Me neither," Paige echoed.

"Yeah, you do," Brother insisted. "Remember? It was back before there were real garbage trucks, back when Mr. Vaughn would drive his pickup from house to house and pick up everybody's trash."

That detail rang a little bitty bell in the back of my head.

"Remember? He would drive from house to house, and nobody had to put their trash at the street or anything, so he'd come down the driveway and have to get out of his truck and grab the garbage cans from behind the house."

"OH, YEAH," Paige, Benji, and I said in unison.

The children's spoons were still suspended in midair.

"Well," Brother said, "since he had to get out of his truck, he had to deal with everybody's dogs. That was before neighborhoods had rules about dogs being inside fences—they were all just free to wander. And since some of those dogs were pretty mean, Mr. Vaughn figured out a way to handle 'em."

Joseph's eyes were as big as Mama's dinner plates. "What'd he do? What'd he do to those dogs?"

"Keep in mind this was back in the early '70s," Brother said. "Back before people put their dogs in sweaters and took 'em to special beauty shops. Dogs were just dogs back then. And since Mr. Vaughn didn't want any of the dogs on our road to bite him, he'd scare 'em off."

"What'd he do? What'd he do to those dogs?" Joseph repeated.

"Aw, nothing *that* bad," Brother answered. "But if he was about to pick up trash at a house where the dogs liked to jump and snarl, he'd turn into the driveway, roll down his window, and throw a few lit firecrackers into the yard. That *KAPOW!* would always make the dogs run. He didn't hurt 'em or anything. Just reminded 'em that he was there. And that's how we could tell that the garbage man was coming—we'd hear *KAPOW! KAPOW! KAPOW!* and know that he was just a few houses away."

The children collapsed into a fit of giggles. The grown-ups did too. And at that point we were off to the story races. Mama and Chox joined us at the table, and one story led to another and another and another. When the kids started to get restless, we moved to the table on the deck and continued the conversation while they ran around the yard, climbed trees, and threw makeshift Frisbees.

The setting was completely different, of course, but in so

many ways and for so many reasons it was like we were sitting in Mamaw and Papaw Davis's kitchen all over again, listening to Mama and Chox and their kinfolk hold court for the better part of an afternoon.

As we sat on the deck and soaked up the sunshine, it dawned on me that it won't be long before my little guy's generation literally and figuratively sits where my generation sits right now—with *their* children and nieces and nephews on the other side of the table. It's sweet to think about that.

And it's sobering.

We live in a world where, if we're honest, we have to admit that people sometimes know more about the Kardashians than they do about the folks who are sleeping right down the hall. In fact, I recently overheard (okay, I was eavesdropping *again*, but I was at Starbucks and the ceilings there are twenty feet tall and the people were talking very loudly) a conversation where two girls were talking about the stars of *Twilight* like they're close, personal friends who regularly hang out together. And I guess I understand why. Anyone who's looking for an unmerited sense of closeness or maybe just an easy way to disconnect from reality can pick up a phone, consult the Google, and spend the better part of an afternoon gathering all manner of interesting trivia about the celebrity obsession of the moment. Considering I personally devoted countless hours of my life to a careful, Internet-based study of Faith Hill's hairstyles in 2001 and 2002, I can speak with some degree of authority on this subject.

The kicker, though, is that God has designed every single one of us for community and for fellowship, and I'm going to go out on a limb and say that usmagazine.com cannot adequately meet that need. But our families? And our friends who feel like family? As Liz Lemon would say on *30 Rock*, THAT IS THE BUSINESS.

As we share our stories with those people God has specifically ordained to walk with us on this side of eternity—and as they share their stories with us—we see the sacred in the ordinary. We see the profound in the mundane. We see the joy in the day to day.

We see the hand of God writing a much bigger story—a story of rescue and redemption and hope and glory. Right here in the middle of the hilarious and the tragic and the sublime and the sad.

That's just something else, isn't it?

After the dishes from Easter lunch were clean and the children were worn slap out, it was time for us to head home to the 'Ham. The sun was just starting to fall behind the treetops, and since we were hoping to be back at our house before dark, we hugged necks and kissed cheeks and said good-bye to our people. Mama and Daddy walked to the car with us, and after Mama and Alex hugged about four more times through his rolled-down window, we backed out of the driveway. We were almost to the end of the street when I looked in my rearview mirror.

And I'll have you know that my mama was still waving.

Bless her.

As we turned onto the road that leads to the highway, I thought about the day and the people and the stories. I thought about how many times I've sat around some family member's table and listened to the latest news, the latest drama, the latest funny tale. I thought about Mama and the hundreds of meals she's planned and cooked just because "the children are gonna be home." I thought about Chox and the countless pots of coffee she's made over the years when we stopped by to visit—and how many times she's called me and said, "What are you doing this weekend? Paige and I may come for a visit. Don't plan anything special, though. We just want to laugh."

And I thought about how, through every stage of my life, my parents, siblings, in-laws, aunts, uncles, and cousins have taught me that family life isn't always easy, and complications are inevitable, and whether you like it or not, sometimes you're going to get your feelings hurt. Sometimes you may even be the one who does the hurting. But you stay with it, and you get after it, and you love each other, and you forgive each other, and you keep coming back to the table.

No matter what. You keep coming back to the table.

And once you're there, you sit down, and you settle in, and you remember. You share your stories.

For the first half of my life, probably, I thought that the whole point of the table was the food. The table was the place to find the fried chicken, deviled eggs, black-eyed peas, and homemade rolls. But now that I'm older, I know better. And it's comforting, somehow, to recognize that while the food may be what brings us to the table, it's not the main course by a long shot. More than anything, I think, the food is an invitation to see what the Lord is doing, to "taste and see that the LORD is good" (Psalm 34:8). Because when people gather around the table to break bread, the Lord gets to work. He knits together our hearts, strengthens our bonds, and connects our narratives. The table is where He links the generations, where He prompts us to join hands and bow heads and remember and laugh and pass our stories back and forth to each other.

Unless, of course, the story requires you to chronicle your aunt Mildred's recent bout with a nasty stomach bug. Because in that case, I'd probably advise that you hold off until every-body's finished their cake and coffee.

But by all means, you feel free to share as the Lord leads.

It's His story, after all.

And Now It Is Time for All the Food

Initially I didn't have any intention of including recipes in this book. However, once I started writing the last few chapters, I thought, *You know, if I read a book that referenced all sorts of tasty Southern food and I didn't have access to the recipes, that might chap my hide a little bit.* And since I certainly don't want you to put this book down and walk away with a chapped hide, I thought it would be a good idea to pass along a few of our family's favorites.

Most of these recipes came from my mama—or from her friends—and I can assure you that you are in wonderful culinary hands. Keep in mind that Mama is exceedingly loyal to her favorite brands, so I'm including those specific brands in the recipes. I'm sure that other brands would work just as well.

However, Mama would want me to include one caveat, and it's something she told me when I was a newlywed: "You might as well go ahead and accept that there is just no substitute for Land O'Lakes butter."

I fought that hard truth for a long time. But she's right.

Enjoy, y'all!

Mama Ouida's Pink Arctic-Freeze Congealed Salad

- 1 (8-ounce) package Philadelphia cream cheese, softened
- 2 tablespoons Hellmann's mayonnaise
- 2 tablespoons sugar
- 1 (16-ounce) can whole berry cranberry sauce
- 1 cup crushed pineapple, drained
- 1 cup heavy cream, whipped

Beat cream cheese, mayonnaise, and sugar in mixer. Add cranberry sauce and pineapple. Mix well. Fold in whipped cream. Freeze in a 9 x 9 dish. Cut into squares to serve.

Poppy-Seed Dressing

- 1½ cups sugar
- 2 teaspoons dry mustard
- 2 teaspoons salt
- ⅔ cup apple cider vinegar
- 3 tablespoons finely grated onion
- 2 cups canola oil
- 3 tablespoons poppy seeds

Mix sugar, mustard, salt, and vinegar in blender. Add onion and blend thoroughly. Add oil slowly, blending constantly, and continue blending until thick. Add poppy seeds and blend for another minute or two. Store in a covered jar in the refrigerator. Serve over fresh fruit.

Makes 2½ cups.

Mama's Deviled Eggs

12 large eggs
1 tablespoon salt (for boiling)
¼ cup Hellmann's mayonnaise
1½ teaspoons Lea & Perrins Worcestershire sauce
1 teaspoon dry mustard
½ teaspoon salt (for filling)
½ teaspoon black pepper
2 tablespoons sweet pickle relish, well drained
3 strips bacon, fried
paprika (for garnish)

Place cold eggs in a boiler filled with cold water. Add a table-spoon of salt and bring to a boil. Boil eggs for five minutes; then turn off heat. Place a lid on the boiler and let sit for 10 minutes. Transfer eggs to a bath of ice water, then peel. Cut eggs in half lengthwise, scoop out yolks, and mix mashed yolks with mayonnaise, Worcestershire sauce, mustard, salt, pepper, and relish. Fill egg whites with yolk mixture, then garnish each deviled egg with ¼ strip bacon and paprika. Serve in your favorite deviled egg dish. OF COURSE.

The Chicken Salad

4 cups chicken breast, cooked and shredded (Mama cooks her chicken breasts in boiling water with salt, pepper, and a few stalks of celery)
juice of 1 lemon
1 Red Delicious apple, grated
3 cups celery, diced very fine
¾ cup sweet pickle relish

1 cup chopped pecans, walnuts, or almonds
½ can drained crushed pineapple (optional)
½ cup Craisins (optional)
1 cup chopped red grapes (optional)
1 cup Hellmann's mayonnaise
1 tablespoon Durkee's Famous Sauce

After you shred the cooked chicken breasts, put the chicken in a large bowl and pour lemon juice over it. Add apple, celery, relish, nuts, and any of the three optional ingredients (usually one of the three ingredients is plenty—we're partial to the chopped red grapes). Mix in mayonnaise and Durkee's, then stir well to combine. Cover and chill.

Note: The salad is better if mixed a day before serving.

Mama's Turkey Divan

2 bunches fresh broccoli, chopped and cooked (it should still be bright green and crunchy)
2–3 cups cooked turkey, diced or sliced (chicken also works great)
2 cans Campbell's cream of chicken soup
1 cup Hellmann's mayonnaise
juice of ½ lemon
1 teaspoon curry powder
1½ tablespoons dry mustard
1 tablespoon Lea & Perrins Worcestershire sauce
1 cup sharp cheddar cheese, grated
½ cup toasted bread crumbs
2 tablespoons Land O'Lakes butter, cut into pats

Lightly grease a 9 x 13 casserole dish with nonstick cooking spray. Place cooked broccoli on the bottom of the dish, then cover with turkey. In a separate bowl, mix together soup, mayonnaise, lemon juice, curry powder, mustard, and Worcestershire sauce. Pour over turkey and broccoli. Cover with cheese. Top with bread crumbs, and then scatter pats of butter over the top. Bake at 350 degrees for 25–30 minutes.

Note: This dish can be made ahead of time and baked when needed.

Edna Holland's Beef Tenderloin

Edna, who is one of my mama's dearest friends and one of my favorite people on the planet, owned a bed-and-breakfast in my hometown for many years. She is an absolutely phenomenal cook, and her cookbook, *Recipes from a Deep South Inn*, was WORN OUT after my first year of marriage. Edna's beef tenderloin recipe is my favorite, and if you don't sop up some of the cooked tenderloin sauce with a warm roll, you are missing out on one of life's great blessings. Absolutely delicious.

> 1 whole beef tenderloin (5–6 pounds)
> salt
> lemon pepper
> cracked black pepper
> A.1. steak sauce
> Lea & Perrins Worcestershire sauce

Trim all fat from tenderloin (or ask your butcher to do so). Three hours before cooking time, place tenderloin in a foil-lined roasting pan and sprinkle each side with salt, lemon pepper, and black

pepper. Pour A.1. and Worcestershire liberally over both sides.
Cover and refrigerate.

Thirty minutes before cooking, place the covered pan on the
counter so the meat isn't quite so cold when you put it in the
oven. Cook at 425 degrees (35 minutes for rare, 40 minutes for
medium, and 45 minutes for well done).

Remove pan from oven and let meat rest 5–10 minutes. Slice.
If using for heavy hors d'oeuvres on a buffet (which is our favorite way to use this recipe), slice thinly and serve with rolls and
assorted spreads.

Squash Casserole

  3 pounds yellow squash
  1 stick Land O'Lakes butter, divided in half
  ½ cup chopped onion, sautéed lightly
  2 eggs, beaten
  1 tablespoon sugar
  1 teaspoon salt
  ½ teaspoon black pepper
  1 cup crushed saltine crackers (very finely crushed)

Wash squash and cook whole in boiling water. Boil until tender,
drain thoroughly, and then mash in a mixing bowl. Add half of
butter, stir, and then add onion, eggs, sugar, salt, and pepper (salt
and pepper may be adjusted to taste). Pour squash mixture into
a lightly greased casserole dish, and then top with finely crushed
crackers. Melt remaining half of butter and pour over cracker
crumbs. Bake at 375 degrees for 45 minutes to an hour—until
golden brown.

My Favorite Chicken and Dumplings

Dumplings

> 2 cups all-purpose flour
> 1 egg, beaten
> 1 teaspoon table salt
> 1 cup buttermilk (if you like fluffy, biscuity dumplings, add
>   2 teaspoons baking powder—but we like dense dumplings
>   around here)

In a mixing bowl, combine flour, beaten egg, salt, and buttermilk. Once mixture is blended, cover the bowl and set aside. Don't overmix—it'll make the dumplings tough.

Chicken Soup

> 2 fully cooked rotisserie chickens
> ½ stick real-live (salted) butter
> ¼ cup all-purpose flour
> 1 (32-ounce) box chicken stock (I like Kitchen Basics)
> 2 cups water
> salt and pepper to taste (don't be bashful with the seasonings)
> 1 teaspoon Worcestershire sauce
> ¼ teaspoon garlic powder
> ¼ cup half-and-half

Pull meat off rotisserie chickens. Chop into cubes and then set aside.

In a Dutch oven, melt butter over low heat. Once all the bubbles are gone, start sprinkling the ¼ cup of flour into the pot. Add a little, stir to combine, then add a little more, stir to combine, etc. Once all the flour has been incorporated, continue to stir over low-to-medium heat until the mixture starts to turn a golden color. You don't want it to get brown—just golden. (It'll only take a couple of minutes.)

Once you see that golden color, start adding liquid to the mixture. Add about a cup of chicken stock and whisk it well so that everything combines. Then add half the water and whisk to combine. Add more chicken stock and whisk. Continue until all the water and stock have been mixed with the flour-and-butter mixture. Turn the heat up to medium and continue to whisk frequently to ensure that you don't have any lumps. (This is a great time to taste the stock mixture, by the way—the butter and stock already have salt, but you'll probably need to add more salt and pepper to taste.)

Let the mixture simmer for about 10 minutes—until it's thicker and not quite so brothy. Add Worcestershire sauce, garlic powder, half-and-half, and chicken. Stir to combine everything, then taste again. Add more salt and pepper if necessary.

Once the whole mixture is simmering and is seasoned just the way you like it, drop the dumpling dough into the pot by spoonfuls. It'll start to look crowded, but that's okay. Once everything is in the pot, let the dumplings simmer (uncovered) for about 15–20 minutes. Once they've cooked through, take the whole pot off the heat, cover it, and leave it alone for about 15–20 minutes.

After 15–20 minutes, take off the lid, grab a ladle, and serve the chicken and dumplings in some oversized bowls.

Amen.

Green Beans Y'all Won't Believe

from *Heart and Soul: Stirring Recipes from Memphis*

½ pound bacon, chopped into bite-size pieces and fried, reserving 3 tablespoons grease
6 cans whole green beans, drained
6 tablespoons sugar
6 tablespoons white vinegar
2 packages slivered almonds

Place drained green beans in a casserole dish. While bacon is draining on paper towels, mix 3 tablespoons bacon grease with sugar and vinegar over medium heat until sugar dissolves and mixture is heated through. Sprinkle bacon on top of green beans, then pour liquid mixture on top and garnish with slivered almonds. Bake at 325 degrees for 25–30 minutes. Then praise God from whom all blessings flow.

Note: I would like to add that the whole draining-the-bacon-on-paper-towels step is pretty much irrelevant since you will be stirring bacon grease into a mixture of vinegar and sugar, but maybe it'll make you feel better to go to the trouble of blotting and draining. Whatever gets you through.

Cornbread Dressing

1 10-inch skillet of cornbread
4 day-old biscuits
1 stick Land O'Lakes butter (melted if the cornbread isn't hot)
1 onion, chopped fine
1 cup celery, chopped fine

1 cup cooked white rice

4 eggs, beaten

6 cups turkey stock or chicken stock

salt and pepper to taste

Make cornbread according to your favorite recipe (I like the White Lily cornbread mix, but Mama goes old school with flour and cornmeal).

In a large mixing bowl, crumble cornbread and biscuits. Add butter, onion, celery, rice, and eggs, then stir to combine. (I like to sauté my onion and celery in a little butter beforehand, but Mama doesn't.) Slowly add stock to the mixture, stirring gently. Add salt and pepper to taste. Some people like to add poultry seasoning or sage, so if that's your thing, go right ahead.

Pour into a buttered 9 x13 casserole dish and bake at 350 for 25–30 minutes or until golden brown on top.

Serve with your favorite gravy or with cranberries. I've even been known to spoon a little homemade plum jelly on top of mine.

Mama's Pound Cake

2 sticks Land O'Lakes butter, softened, plus additional butter for tube pan

½ cup Crisco

3 cups sugar

5 eggs

3 cups Swan's Down cake flour

1 cup whole milk

1½ teaspoons pure vanilla extract

½ teaspoon baking powder

Butter and flour a tube pan. With an electric mixer, combine butter and Crisco until light and fluffy—about 3–4 minutes. Slowly add sugar as you continue to mix, and then add eggs one at a time, making sure each one has combined before adding the next one. Starting with flour, alternate incorporating flour and milk, making sure to end with flour. Add vanilla, then turn off mixer and stir in baking powder with a fork (Mama insists on stirring in the baking powder with a fork, so use a spoon at your peril). Pour batter into tube pan and place in a cold oven. Bake for about 1½ hours at 325 degrees (cooking time will vary depending on your oven).

Pumpkin Spice Cake

   3 eggs
   1¼ cups sugar
   1 cup canned pumpkin (not pumpkin pie filling)
   ½ cup vegetable oil
   ½ cup water
   1¾ cups all-purpose flour, sifted
   1 teaspoon salt
   ¾ teaspoon baking soda
   2 teaspoons cinnamon
   1 teaspoon nutmeg
   1 cup quick rolled oats, uncooked

Beat eggs until frothy, and then add sugar gradually. Beat until thick and lemon colored. Stir in pumpkin, oil, and water. Blend well. In a separate bowl, mix together flour, salt, baking soda, cinnamon, and nutmeg. Add gradually to pumpkin mixture, blending well. Stir in oats. Pour into a well-greased, floured

9 x 13 pan. Bake at 350 degrees for about 30 minutes. Loosen edges with knife or spatula. Cool 10 minutes, and then invert on serving plate. Cool completely. Ice with orange butter frosting.

Orange Butter Frosting

    2 tablespoons butter
    2½ cups confectioners' sugar
    3 tablespoons orange juice
    1 teaspoon orange peel, grated
    pinch of salt

Cream butter. Add sugar gradually, alternating with enough orange juice to make the frosting the right consistency for spreading. Stir in orange peel and salt.

Mamaw Davis's Chocolate Pudding

    ¾ cup sugar
    3 heaping tablespoons all-purpose flour
    2 heaping tablespoons cocoa powder (I like Hershey's)
    2 eggs
    2 egg yolks (that's not a typo—that would be 4 egg yolks
        total, or two days' worth of your recommended cholesterol
        intake)
    2 cups whole milk
    2 tablespoons Land O'Lakes butter
    2 teaspoons pure vanilla extract

In a medium-size saucepan (no heat yet), stir together sugar, flour, and cocoa powder until there are no lumps. (I actually run mine through a sifter, but hey, I'm high maintenance.)

In a separate bowl, beat the eggs and egg yolks.

Fold eggs and egg yolks into dry mixture.

Once eggs are fully incorporated, add milk. Stir until combined, and then turn on stove to a medium-high heat. You don't want to boil this custard, so be careful you don't have too much heat going or the pudding will curdle.

Stir or whisk mixture constantly until it starts to thicken—about 10 minutes. Remove from heat and stir in butter and vanilla.

Makes 4–6 servings, which I pour immediately into individual dessert bowls. (It cools quicker that way.)

Note: This pudding is also a great pie filling. Just bake the pie crust according to instructions, add filling, whip up some meringue, lightly brown meringue, and prepare for the undying devotion of your family and friends.

Acknowledgments

To Bill Jensen, agent and encourager extraordinaire, for sharing wisdom, offering guidance, and clinging to a deep, steady reverence for what the Lord does around the table.

To Stephanie Rische, for praying faithfully, recognizing that I really do say "the Google," and making this book so much better through your loving attention to detail.

To Lisa Jackson and the Tyndale team, for believing in these stories, tolerating my love for ALL CAPS (and parentheses), and seeing what I couldn't. It has been my joy to work with you.

To Emma Kate, Laura, Marion, Elizabeth, Melissa, Daphne, Elise, Tracey, Wendi, and Katy, for being the reasons why I don't understand mean girls. You are the sweetest, most supportive, most hilarious friends on earth. And you've encouraged me to write since I was nineteen and prone to things like impromptu perms and crispy bangs. I love y'all.

To Melanie, for walking arm-in-arm through unchartered territory these last seven years. It has been an adventure, my friend, and I'm so thankful that the Lord knew we'd need each other. I look forward to many more years of blog therapy, SEC analysis, and podcast technical difficulties. You are the best gift the Internet has ever given me.

To my blogger friends, for keeping my feed reader full, for writing so beautifully, for having big, wide-open hearts, and for making me laugh and think. A lot.

To the sweetest blog readers anyone could want, for showing up every day and never complaining when I post about football—AGAIN. Your prayers and e-mails and comments have spurred me on, and when I say that there never would have been a book without you, I mean it. I am grateful from the bottom of my heart.

To Mrs. Reynolds, Mrs. Scarborough, Mrs. Robbins, Mrs. Bruckmeier, and Dr. Hargrove, for teaching so well and grading so thoughtfully. You are amazing, gifted women, and I am forever indebted to you.

To my BCS family, for serving selflessly, working tirelessly, and making much of Jesus every single day. Your courage and your dedication inspire me. And also: you are really stinkin' funny. I have never stopped thanking God for you.

To Dr. K and Mary Jo, for welcoming us to Birmingham with open arms. Your servant-hearted example has impacted our family in ways you may never know this side of heaven. You are such a blessing to us!

To Wednesday night Bible study, for teaching and listening and praying and loving. I'm so grateful for each one of you.

To Sister, for remembering, well, *everything* and filling in my memory gaps (in great detail, I might add). You have given me a love for finding the funny in the middle of the ordinary ("I like mustard on my crackers"), and you tell stories better than I could ever write them. That's the truth. Hail State and Go 'Dogs.

To my big ole family (the one I was born into and the one I married), for teaching me how to love and to laugh, for sharing your unwavering faith, and for insisting that we make time for the table. Thank you for trusting me to tell our stories. I love y'all so much.

To Alex, for stealing my heart and multiplying my joy. You are a source of endless delight to your daddy and me, and I am so tickled that I get to be your mama. You make me proud every single day, and when I think about how I wrote a big chunk of this book with you sitting beside me, it makes my heart smile.

To David, for being steady, patient, and supportive (which is so helpful considering that I can err on the side of being a white-hot mess-o-crazy). Plus, you make me laugh every single day. Well, almost. Not so much on the days when you sing that line from that Jason Aldean song approximately 602 times. But other than that: ACES. I love you.

And finally, to Jesus: "E'er since, by faith, I saw the stream Thy flowing wounds supply / Redeeming love has been my theme, and shall be till I die."

About the Author

With an urge to document the hilarity of family life, **Sophie Hudson** began writing her blog in November 2005. Since then she has seen her blog readership grow beyond what she would have thought possible. Sophie hopes that through her stories, women will find encouragement and hope in the everyday, joy-filled moments of life. In addition to her blog, BooMama.net, Sophie writes on a regular basis for *HomeLife* magazine and is a regular contributor to the Pioneer Woman's blog. She also serves as co-emcee for LifeWay's annual dotMOM event and partici-pates in Compassion International's blogger initiative. Sophie lives with her husband and son in Birmingham, Alabama.